THE COHERENCE CODE

How to Maximize Your Performance and Success in Business

For Individuals, Teams, and Organizations

Robert Keith Wallace, PhD, Ted Wallace, MS, Samantha Wallace

ISBN 978-0-9990558-5-4

Library of Congress Control Number: 2019917567

DharmaPublications.com

Dharma Publications, Fairfield, IA

To Our Very Dear Children and Grandchildren

THIS IS THE COMPANION BOOK TO:

Total Brain Coaching

A Holistic System of Effective Habit Change
For the Individual, Team, and Organization

Ted Wallace, MS, Robert Keith Wallace, PhD, Samantha Wallace

Contents

CAST OF CHARACTERS

MR. SMITH

The main character, Mr. J.P. Smith, first appeared in *Quantum Golf* published in 1991. [Note to Reader: Mr. Smith is also the star of our latest book *Beauty And Being Yourself.*]

Smith's initials, J.P., stand for John Paul. Under no circumstances, however, does he allow anyone other than his wife Margaret to use his given name. And even she usually uses only his initials. Margaret has been the love of Mr. Smith's life since they met in college. The couple has a grown son, a daughter-in-law, and two grandchildren.

The Smiths live in the penthouse apartment of an old Upper East Side New York apartment building. Mr. Smith is a typical busy businessman, who founded SMITH & HATHAWAY with Margaret's father, Robert Hathaway. Compulsively focused at all times, Smith's great obsession is being on time, while his enduring ambition is to improve his golf game.

[Note to Reader: Mr. Smith's frequent use of the admittedly coarse words "frak" and "fraking" has nothing to do with the environmentally unfriendly process of hydraulic fracturing to obtain oil and gas, commonly known as fracking. It is merely the result of his viewing all 76 episodes of the television show Battlestar Galactica 7 times, and counting.]

MARGARET

It is generally agreed that Smith hit the jackpot in his choice of wife. Margaret's characteristic empathy, strong intellect, sense of responsibility, refinement, and her contentment with life, tends to have a harmonizing influence on the entire family. Most people (and animals) sense Margaret's deeply grounded nature and feel safe around her.

LINC ST. CLAIRE

A mystical golf teacher who is featured in *Quantum Golf*

DAME GEORGINA ST. GEORGE

Linc St. Claire's cousin, who is an extraordinary business consultant sought after by the very rich and powerful

DOUG HATCHETT

CEO of SMITH & HATHAWAY

BEN ARNOLD

President of SMITH & HATHAWAY

(Note to Reader: The President is under the CEO and head of operations for the company.)

ANNE BRIGHT

Chief in-house legal counsel of SMITH & HATHAWAY

HAMILTON JR.

Son of major stockholder in SMITH & HATHAWAY, consultant working at Boston Consulting, new employee of SMITH & HATHAWAY

PAUL GREEDLEY

Past CEO of SMITH & HATHAWAY and now head of a competing firm

SERAPHIM

Margaret's older sister and an arch nemesis of J.P. Smith. She is a wealthy widow whose deepest desire is to control...the world. Or at the very least, to control and guide the members of her family with what she considers a benevolent hand.

CHAPTER 1

THE COHERENCE CODE

The Way to Succeed through Holistic Habit Change

A t 7:55 AM, J.P. Smith, the founder and chairman of the board of one of largest sporting equipment companies in the US, steps out of his sedan to the distant wail of sirens. He is already tired as he slams the door dispiritedly behind him. In the reflection of the car's multi-layered lacquer finish, the gray of his suit slides down into the cement at his feet.

Throwing his head back like a drowning man, Smith looks up. Searching amidst the towering tops of buildings for a patch of sky, he finds it. It too is gray.

He slowly climbs the stone steps to the Wall Street office building his company has occupied for nearly 50 years. Glancing at the engraved words SMITH & HATHAWAY in the polished brass plaque, his usual feeling of general satisfaction is mixed with apprehension. He reaches out his hand to push the revolving door in front of him, but before he can lean into it, the siren sounds become noticeably louder. Glancing down the street, he sees two motorcycle cops riding in front of a dark blue stretch limo. Flags flutter on either side of the massive vehicle.

Who could it be, he muses, welcoming the momentary distraction, *some sheik, Asian potentate? A movie star? Pork belly king?* This was, after all, Wall Street.

Immediately below, the cavalcade draws to a stop and security men leap from the car, all wearing discreet earphones.

The two policemen, still mounted on their mechanical beasts, stare blankly at him through mirrored sunglasses. One security guy opens the rear door of the limo and the rest go on red alert as a slender feminine figure wearing a finely tailored ivory suit and sunglasses steps out of the car. Her security detail clusters around her like anxious bees. Waving them away, the lady energetically mounts the steps in Smith's direction, and as she reaches him, she extends her hand.

"J.P. Smith, I presume?"

Nodding mutely, he shakes her proffered hand.

"Allow me to introduce myself," she says. "My formal title is Dame Georgina St. George. My cousin, Linc St. Claire, asked me to see you."

The sound of her low honeyed voice confounds him and for a long moment he is speechless.

This, he thinks, *is Georgie, the world-class management consultant and expert on the ins and outs of mergers and acquisitions that Linc told me about at our golf lesson yesterday. He did not, however, mention that Georgie is a woman!*

He stutters, "H-h-how did you get here so fast?"

"Linc told me about the problems your company is having and

since my trip to Africa this morning was canceled—the people having called for general election," she says as an aside—"it seems that nature has rearranged my calendar and provided the opportune moment for me to address your situation." An enigmatic smile plays on her gleaming red lips.

'Nature' rearranged her calendar? he thinks. *She sure sounds like Linc.*

Belatedly he notices she is waiting for him to speak. "Ah, well, the thing is," he hurries on, "I'm not really sure how you can help."

She laughs, "I've already started. After studying your annual reports, I called friends at a few banks to learn if anyone from your competitor, Greedley, had approached them for financing. Then I did some research on Superflex. I must say they are an excellent fit for your company. Their new golf shafts, along with a couple of their other high-tech products, could revolutionize the golf industry. Acquiring them would be a perfect strategic move for you to shift your image from a conventional sports company to a specialty golf company on the bleeding edge of sports technology!

"However," she says, holding up a manicured hand, "Superflex is seriously considering Greedley's proposal. A new board member is driving the acquisition, and apparently money is no obstacle."

Smith squints at her. "I see. Well," he says tightly, "thanks." *One thing is for sure, she has excellent sources of information.*

He nods to the imposing brassbound glass doors. "Come in, please. My executive management team is about to meet."

"I'll be delighted to meet your people," she smiles, and together they take the elevator to the 38th floor.

Smith's imposing office has a spectacular ceiling-to-floor view and an ancient but still beautiful vegetable-dyed carpet. Chosen years ago by Smith's wife, it lies beside an oval conference table of clouded maple. Large photographs of three of America's greatest historic golf champions, Bobby Jones, Sam Snead, and Ben Hogan, hang on the wall opposite the window. Below the images, four antique hickory wood golf clubs rest in individual cases. A small group of wing chairs cluster amicably around Smith's old rosewood desk in the far corner of the room. In the opposite corner, there is an indoor putting cup, a small bucket of golf balls, and a putter.

Drawing a chair for Georgina, and one for himself, Smith addresses his already seated team. "I want you all to meet Dame Georgina St. George. Dame Georgina is an international consultant here at my invitation."

The room is silent for several moments. Doug Hatchett, a red-haired six-foot-five giant, and the company's CEO, is the first to speak. "We heard rumors that Greedley was interested in Superflex, but no one took it seriously because the guy had no significant capital. We are as surprised as you are. Suddenly the banks are in love with him and are fighting to finance his new acquisition."

Smith is calm. Not happy, but calm.

"I know," Hatchett continues, "that it's bad timing, but Westport Consulting is scheduled to make a presentation right now regarding our managerial practices. They've been interviewing our employees for weeks and Hamilton Ridgeway Sr.'s son, as you know, is one of their members. They're waiting in the other room," he said, tilting his head in that direction.

Since Hamilton Ridgeway Sr. happens to be one of SMITH & HATHAWAY's major stockholders, the issue is mildly sensitive.

"Of course," Hatchett goes on, "we could always tell them that we have an emergency and postpone the meeting."

Smith chews his thumbnail. *This is no time to show weakness.* "Call them in!" he says decisively.

Moments later, two men and one woman, led by Hamilton Ridgeway Jr., enter the room. A taller blonder version of his bald dad, he is sturdy and athletic. The young man radiates a bright peaceful friendliness.

Dame St. George smiles at him and receives a wide dimpled grin in return.

Westport Consulting's status report makes SMITH & HATHAWAY sound like a terminal patient with a long list of ailments, beginning with the undeniable fact that the company has been losing customers to more aggressive and technologically savvy firms for some time. The report even mentions an outbreak of employee theft, which Smith takes as a personal affront.

The Westport group also brings up SMITH & HATHAWAY's employee net promoter score, which is a -30. *Even our own employees,* Smith thinks bitterly, *are not recommending our products!*

The meeting draws to a merciful close after almost a full hour, and everyone, except for Smith and the good Dame, files out of the room.

At this point, Smith is feeling almost ill with fatigue and concern. "I'm sorry I wasted your time, Dame Georgina. We're in worse shape than I could have imagined. It hasn't been that long since I retired. I knew that things were slipping but I didn't realize that it had come to this."

Holding his head in his hands, he tells her, "I feel like a fool for thinking that the acquisition of Superflex was all we needed to take us over the top."

"First of all," she says briskly, "call me Georgina. Secondly, I didn't want to speak during the presentation," she says, "but, my dear Mr. Smith, your situation is far from irresolvable. In my view, the company has only one serious problem."

He looks at her in disbelief. "Did we just hear the same report? The list of problems is a mile long!"

"Yes," she smiles, "it's quite a list, but," she shrugs, "they are solvable problems. The crux of the situation is that SMITH & HATHAWAY lacks coherence."

"Excuse me; we're in a sinking ship, surrounded by a feeding frenzy of sharks, and," he says in disbelief, "you're saying that our main problem is that we aren't coherent?"

The consultant stands up and strolls over to the window, where she picks up the putter leaning against the wall. "Westport raised important considerations, which, of course, must be dealt with practically."

"I'm glad we agree on something," says Smith.

"Oh, indeed," she agrees, scooping up a golf ball lying beside the indoor putting cup. "The solution to your problems lies in something I call The Coherence Code."

"Is that like the Da Vinci Code?" he asks.

Instead of answering, she walks about 10 feet away, drops the ball, and lines up the putter. Smith watches as she pauses to breathe, and slowly strokes the ball, which rolls dead center into the hole.

Georgina looks at him and says, "The Coherence Code is the way to succeed through effective habit change. I'll teach you how improve the habits of individuals, teams, and the company as a whole, aligning their mindset and goals. This will create coherence in the culture of a company. You will see an evolution of vision, strategy, structure, systems, processes, and people."

My business is falling apart and she's talking about some secret code!

"Right now," she explains, "SMITH & HATHAWAY is having what can be compared to a mental breakdown. Think of a company as having a mind, a corporate mind, which is simply the sum of the collection of individual minds that form the company."

"Wait a minute," he says, "so you are telling me that it's this corporate mindset thing that's causing all our problems?"

"When there is incoherence in the individual minds of the employees and management, when there are bad habits at every level in the organization, the corporate mindset of a company becomes weak and vulnerable. It is then both natural and inevitable for fear and mistakes to arise.

"The top five companies in the world—Amazon, Apple, Facebook, Google, and Microsoft —all have a coherent and agile mindset, which is why they are able to adapt so quickly to the customer's needs."

Smith asks, "What exactly do you mean when you use the word 'coherence'?"

"Coherence is usually understood as a state in which there are orderly relationships between the parts of a system. When you watch a migrating flock of Canada geese, one of the first things you notice is that their formation or shape is never static. It is in a dynamic state of order, altering to take different conditions into account, always maintaining the most efficient pattern."

Georgina continues, "There are also many examples from physics. Consider a laser beam. The reason it has such power is that all of its light waves are of the same amplitude and phase. In other words, they are perfectly harmonious and coherent with each other. As a result, a laser can slice through the hardest metal and send a beam of light to the moon. Similarly, when every individual in a company begins to function in a highly coherent and harmonious manner, there is virtually nothing their company cannot accomplish."

Smith's brain reels.

"Coherence," she tells him, "can be seen everywhere in nature, from the growth of the smallest flower to the vast and precise rotation of the planets."

Sounds more like space travel than business management! thinks Smith.

"Your body," she continues, "is one of the best examples of the power of coherence. Let's imagine your many cells as the employees in a very large corporation. Each of the teams and departments are like tissues, organs, and systems, and each has a different function. For example, some cells in your liver detoxify chemicals, while other liver cells regulate metabolism. Each cell works in a coordinated manner with the cells nearby and with all the other cells in the body. When any cell becomes incoherent, it loses connection with the body as a whole. Cancer is an example of incoherence. When the DNA in a cell becomes significantly damaged, it can become cancerous. The cancerous cell then divides unchecked and is no longer in alignment with the whole of the body."

I sure don't want that kind of incoherence in my body or my company! Smith thinks to himself.

Georgina retrieves the ball from the putting cup and walks to the other end of the room. He watches as she visibly composes herself before knocking another ball right into the cup.

His mouth opens slightly. *If this lady can make my company perform as well as she can putt, we have nothing to worry about!*

"If I go along with this coherence thing, how soon can we see results?"

The Dame raises arched eyebrows. "That depends."

Aha! She's making no guarantees. I knew it was too good to be true!

"It's because of you, Mr. Smith, that SMITH & HATHAWAY was so successful for so long. But now you have introduced new leadership, and, quite frankly, they are creating cracks in the coherence of your company."

He holds up his hands. "Don't get me wrong, Georgina, your comments about our current leadership are spot on. My CEO

Hatchett keeps on complaining. According to him, our problems are everyone else's fault. It's sad, because he's really an excellent strategic thinker. And our president, Ben Arnold, is a solid operations man. The problem is that Ben's behaving as if we're already defeated. He actually comes right out and says how unhappy he is with his job and that it's time for him to move on. Can you imagine? At a time like this, he wants to leave!"

A clear image of rats leaving a sinking ship flashes into his mind.

"Hatchett and Arnold are constantly trying to one-up each other!" he tells her. "They're running around trying to make a name for themselves, the sort of profile stuff they're hoping might make front page of the *Wall Street Journal*. I'm sure their example inspires more infighting than teamwork."

"Clearly, Mr. Smith, it's time for a new coach, one who is able to inspire harmony in your team."

"You want me to fire both my CEO and president?"

"I'm not advising you to fire anyone right now but there are times when it's necessary to cut out dry rot in order to stop it spreading. What I am saying is that your company needs reorganization at the top."

"Such as?"

"A new leader."

He tries not to raise his voice. "Oh, come on. It's not like you're talking about replacing a high school coach! We're a large corporation with thousands of employees. Who am I supposed to find out of the blue to run it?"

"You," she tells him, taking him by surprise.

"Me?" Again he gapes at her.

Shutting his mouth, he swallows slowly. "It took me a long time to give up control of my company. Besides, I thought that it needed fresh, up-to-date management. That's why I hired Greedley two years ago. But he caused no end of problems so I fired him. Now he's my competition!"

"Nevertheless," she says, "it is you who must run the company until it gets back on its feet again."

"Pff! Impossible!" he protests. "I'd have to spend weeks preparing."

"A new company needs a champion, a visionary. Once the company is running well, it's fine to replace the visionary with other leaders who will keep the success going and build on it. Your company has lost faith in its leaders; there's no inspiration, no vision. But your employees trust you! They believed in your original vision and you only have to re-inspire them. It's time for you to reboot SMITH & HATHAWAY."

"I may have been a champion once," he says wearily, "but no one is going to want to follow a geezer like me today."

Her next words surprise him. "You're wrong. Look at Tiger Woods—everyone thought that he was through after all his surgery and other problems, but at the age of 43 he came back to win the Masters. Many older athletes are performing at very high levels. Think of Jack Nicklaus in the 1986 Masters. When he was 46, Nicklaus shot a 30 on the back nine to win. In sports terminology, we could say that he was 'in the zone,' exhibiting a highly coherent state of mind-body coordination.

"Your employees will follow you as long as you create group coherence. And you can do that using The Coherence Code."

"What is this mysterious secret code anyway?"

"The essence of The Coherence Code is discovering your Energy State. For any management program to succeed it is first necessary to understand who you are and how you can improve. This applies to the individual, team, and company as a whole. Unless you have a system in place that provides continuous learning and improvement, there is no chance for higher performance and success.

"The Coherence Code uses a specific system called Total Brain Coaching to help each individual and team understand their strengths and weaknesses and change their habits. A holistic habit change plan can help maintain the balance of your Energy State. If your employees' Energy States are in balance, they will have greater resources to contribute to their individual, team, and organizational goals. They will all have a coherent mindset."

Reaching again for the putter, she gives a quick look in the direction of a second cup near the door. She then hits the ball smoothly and Smith watches the little white orb miss the cup by two or three feet, careening out the open door and down the hall. *Aha!* he crows to himself, *the first sign of fallibility.*

"Take an example from sports," she goes on. "The need for coherence and coordination within a sports team is well known. One of the best examples was the 1969 Boston Celtics basketball team. They were tied with the Los Angeles Lakers for the National Basketball Association championship. The Lakers had three of their all-time greatest players—Elgin Baylor, Jerry West, and Wilt Chamberlain. The final game was in Los Angeles at the Forum, where the Celtics had not won a game all season. Nobody thought the Celtics could win. The Lakers owner, Jack Kent Cooke, was so convinced his team would win that he ordered thousands of balloons with 'World Champion Lakers' printed on them. On every seat there was a flyer that said, 'When, not if, the Lakers win the title, balloons will be released from the rafters, and the USC marching band will play the song *Happy Days Are Here Again!*'

"Bill Russell, who was acting as the Celtics player and coach, got word of the balloons and told his team in no uncertain words that they had to win. And they did. With amazing teamwork the Celtics beat the Lakers and won the championship."

Now she takes a small notebook from her purse, opens it at a particular page, and hands it to him. "Read the underlined quote."

Smith reads:

> I played because I enjoyed it—but there's more to it than that. I played because I was dedicated to being the best. I was part of a team, and I dedicated myself to making that team the best. To me, one of the most beautiful things to see is a group of men coordinating their efforts toward a common goal—alternately subordinating and asserting themselves to achieve real teamwork in action. I tried to do that—we all tried to do that—on the Celtics. I think we succeeded. Often, in my mind's eye, I stood off and watched that effort. I found it beautiful to watch. It's just as beautiful to watch in things other than sports. —Bill Russell

"Tell me, Mr. Smith, what's the first thing a team owner thinks about when his team becomes incoherent?"

"Selling it?"

"Yes, but let's say you want to keep the team," she replies.

"Then," Smith says, "get a new coach or manager!"

"Yes, he knows that his team needs new leadership. It needs a new vision of possibilities to inspire and enliven every member of the team. Most athletes who have been on a long losing streak are only too happy to get a new coach, even though they know it will probably mean reorganization, with some players traded or moved according to the vision of the new coach. These sorts of changes aren't necessarily due to the failure of an individual's performance, but they fit in with the overall needs and requirements of the new coach."

Georgina pauses before continuing. "If you are the coach of your business again, you may well decide to do some reorganizing. Right now your employees are still playing the game, but only for themselves. Each one of them is a valuable resource if they are properly placed and given the tools to build corporate coherence."

Before he can respond, Caroline, his nun-like assistant of twenty years, bursts into the room. "I'm so sorry for interrupting, but there's an urgent call for you."

Smith picks up the heavy landline phone, turning to Georgina. "Do you mind?" he asks with perfunctory courtesy.

"Not at all," she replies.

"Excellent."

He speaks into the phone, "That's exactly what I wanted to know. Thanks."

He hangs up, his face flushed as he looks at Georgina. "I've just learned that Greedley is going to meet with his angel investor at a resort on Kauai next week. And I'm going to be there to deal with them!"

She frowns slightly. "This may not be the wisest course of action right now, Mr. Smith."

Ignoring her, he speeds on, "There's nothing like direct confrontation. I'll expose Greedley in front of his investor!"

He continues enthusiastically, "I promised Margaret, anyway, that I would take our daughter-in-law and the two grandkids on a vacation while our son's away on business. They'll all have a blast in Kauai."

He laughs, "With my grandkids running around, Greedley will never imagine that I'm there to sabotage him!"

Georgina tries again, "You might want to talk the idea over with your wife first."

"No, no, no," he shakes his head. "No time! I'm sorry to cut our meeting short, Georgina, but I have to arrange everything immediately."

Smith accompanies the silent Dame out the door and down the hall. As they walk, the memory of her missed putt comes to mind and he chuckles to himself, but keeps a straight face. *That putt must have gone a good 2 or 3 feet wide of its mark! Haha!*

With his ego fortified by the proof that even Georgina isn't perfect, he thinks fondly, What a good Dame she is.

As they approach another putting cup at the far end of the hall, he sees a new Titleist ball nestled in its center. *What!* he freaks. *Georgina sank a 25 foot putt into a cup she couldn't possibly have seen!*

He is about to reluctantly congratulate her when Caroline again rushes over to him. "There's another urgent call."

"I can't be disturbed now," he growls. "I'm planning a trip."

"Of course, sir," she says, "but it's urgent. Umm, super urgent!"

"Tell them to fraking call back!"

"The call," she says timidly, "is not for you, it's for Dame Georgina St. George. It's the White House. They haven't been able to reach her on her cell phone."

Smith gasps, "The White House is calling?"

"The White House," she confirms.

Georgina says quietly, "I had my cell phone turned off during the meeting and left your office number in case of emergency. I hope you don't mind the intrusion."

"No, no, no, no," he denies fervently. "Of course not!"

She turns her cell phone on and her rose-colored fingertips tap at the screen. The phone rings once before being picked up at the other end of the line. She speaks into the phone, "St. George here."

After a brief pause, she says, "Ah, Mr. President."

Smith can't believe his ears. Georgina continues, "I wonder if I could call you back, Mr. President? I'm a bit tied up with an important matter just now."

His jaw drops all the way open now, like a carp gasping for air.

"Fine," she continues, "I will call you in half an hour."

Pocketing her phone, she turns to Smith. "Any further questions?"

Smith shakes his head, "no." But the odds of his applying The Coherence Code to his company are now 100%.

CHAPTER 2

GAME OF SWORDS

Losing to Learn

Morning sun pours into a spacious bedroom. "J.P.?" Smith recognizes his wife's voice. "Better get up, dear, it's nearly time to go."

Surf roars in the background while he blinks, trying to focus his thoughts. Vaguely, he remembers landing on Kauai last night with the family, and evidently they've spent the night in a beautiful beach cottage.

Today, he thinks, I'm going to catch Greedley with his big whale investor! Suddenly he's sharply awake.

Greedley. Anticipation turns to anxiety. *Good grief, what time is it?* His jet lag isn't helping matters.

As he quickly showers, thoughts of a coming battle make his spirits soar.

Out on the patio, Margaret has ordered a breakfast of ripe tropical fruit, homemade granola, and fresh orange juice, for herself and the grandchildren, Sam, an energetic seven year old, and granddaughter Sky, a precocious five year old.

A large pot of steaming hot organic Kona Teaberry coffee awaits J.P. Daughter-in-law Kara is already enjoying her first cup.

" 'The breakfast of champions!' " Margaret announces cheerily as Smith appears.

Sure, sure, he thinks sourly, sitting down. His brow wrinkles as he squeezes lime halves over wedges of sunset-colored papaya. He is feeling a little guilty about using their family vacation as a front to save the company. But only a little. *I'm sure they'll all understand and applaud once my task is accomplished!*

Buoyed by this thought, he is pleased with himself and carves a perfect golden mound of papaya with his spoon. He brings it up to his mouth but before he can take a bite, the noise of a helicopter shreds the morning peace.

Louder, louder, louder, it approaches. Big blades whip the air as the machine descends.

"Margaret!" he screams over the resounding THUP, THUP! "What is the helicopter doing on the front lawn?"

Napkins whirl off the table, and grass cuttings, like a cloud of thin green bugs, create an unwelcome garnish on his papaya. He tries not to panic. *The thing is practically on top of us!*

His wife speaks very loudly into his ear. "This is our transportation, dear, to take us to the Kyoto Resort! It's on a remote part of the island with no roads. Our bags have gone on ahead."

Meanwhile, Sam and Sky are pretending to be human helicopters, hurling themselves around in circles, knocking over chairs and coming close to toppling a 300-year-old bonsai tree from its carved stone stand.

The big blades circle for several seconds in near silence before coming to a halt. The door to the helicopter opens and a tanned, fit young pilot ducks out.

"Hi!" he calls, removing his cap. "All set to go?"

"We sure are!" Margaret replies.

One by one, the Smiths climb into the helicopter. When everybody's seat belts are fastened, the pilot instructs them to put on their headsets and the engine sound becomes louder as the big bird begins to rise.

"We'll be taking the scenic route up the Hanalei Valley and over to Kilohana Crater." The man's voice is clear through the earphones. "From there we'll fly above the Napali coast to the Kyoto Resort."

The beach below gives way to a cultivated valley and before long they are passing over the edge of the large crater, like an exotic bowl at the heart of Kauai. Silver waterfalls thread vertically down the concave walls and Smith watches mesmerized, as the shadow of their helicopter passes through a rainbow and crosses the crater.

Near the top of one of the innumerable knife-edged emerald mountains, they approach a clearing completely isolated from any other settlement. As they begin to descend, Smith is able to distinguish some of the features of the resort. Tennis courts are in evidence, with a variety of grass, clay, and concrete surfaces. A passionate golfer for his entire adult life, he is particularly pleased to catch sight of the beautiful golf course. There is also a good-sized golf practice area, with a range and a large putting green separated from the tennis courts by what looks like a primeval forest.

There is one main T-shaped building constructed of large blocks of what he will later learn is prehistoric coral. Above and behind this edifice, individual cottages are staggered on an incline, each discreetly screened from its neighbor by a mass of verdant foliage, and each with an ocean view. A short distance away is a promontory overlooking the sea, with a wooden gazebo surrounded by a beautifully laid out Japanese garden. And lower on the mountain horses graze, looking like miniature figurines.

At least at this distance, Smith thinks with approval, *this club or spa, or retreat, whatever it is, appears to be a first-class operation!*

After a remarkably soft landing, the pilot escorts the family into the clubhouse. The first thing Smith notices are huge golden Koa wood beams overhead; he looks around at the scrolls of exquisite calligraphy on the eggshell white walls. For a moment, one ancient brown ink sketch of the seated figure of a monk catches his eye, then, at the front desk, he notices a fine old samurai sword in a plain glass case.

"Ahh, Mr. J.P. Smith!" An enormous young Hawaiian—who could, Smith thinks, have easily made a living as a Sumo wrestler—appears from behind a rosewood shoji screen. "We are very glad to welcome you and your family to the Kyoto Resort."

Coming around to the front of the desk, he bows. "I am Theodore Kumu, assistant manager. How do you do?" Politely, he inclines his head towards each family member in turn.

J.P. nods and Margaret responds with a smile, although her eyes soon wander towards the various art objects in the room. The younger Smiths giggle, "Hi!"

Theodore addresses the Smith patriarch. "We shall take special care of your wife and daughter-in-law and your fine grandchildren while you are here. We have an extensive health spa and a very good art and sport program."

As he escorts them through open sliding doors to a glassed-in dining area, the helicopter can be heard receding in the distance. When everyone is comfortably seated, two graceful Hawaiian women approach and garland them with sweet smelling leis. Tall beaded glasses filled with the juice of freshly beheaded green coconuts are set in front of them.

Smith is starting to relax when a man standing beside the assistant manager captures his attention. *There's something unusual,* he thinks, *something special about this guy. He exudes the condensed energy of a coiled steel spring.*

The man appears to be Japanese, but his eyes are blue in brilliant contrast to his golden skin. *Not the blue of the ocean or the sky,* Smith decides as the two men approach, *but the blue of the hottest part of a flame.*

He can't help staring. *The guy could be any age between thirty and eighty!* The man's craggy face is unlined, but there is something ancient in its timelessness.

"Mr. John Paul Smith and honored family." This time Mr. Kumu makes a more formal bow. "May I present the manager of the Kyoto Resort, Matsuki Hatori San."

Inclining his head, Hatori San extends a strong, well-formed hand, clasping Smith's in a cool grip. "I understand," he says in a deep and serious voice, "that you are on a mission." Then quite unexpectedly, he laughs. Uproariously.

The burst of loud good-natured laughter startles the family. They've never heard such freedom in a laugh. And the mirth is infectious. They all laugh and giggle and roar along with the stranger. Smith coughs to cover his own hilarity. *After all, what does this guy know about my mission?*

Hatori's blue eyes engage him. "You and I, Mr. Smith, will now participate in an activity which will only briefly separate you from your beautiful family."

"Ah, oh-kay," agrees Smith. With a nod to his family, as if everything is going exactly as planned, he follows the man past the lobby and through another door that leads outside to a pine-enclosed garden.

Beyond the trees, he sees a flat lake-shaped stretch of raked sand. And in the middle of the sand there is a shoulder-height wooden platform.

Hatori motions for Smith to follow him up some rock steps. Stepping onto the wooden deck, he experiences a feeling of distinct unease as he notices that Hatori has somehow materialized a pair of gleaming silver swords.

Swords? SWORDS! The guy must have picked them up between the clubhouse and the garden!

But it was only a short walk, how could he have missed it? There is no time to consider the mystery because Hatori promptly hands him one of the swords. Wielding the other with ease, the man assumes a two-handed fighting stance directly in front of him.

Hatori bows yet again. "So, Mr. Smith," he says pleasantly, "your mission begins."

Without another word, he wields his sword overhead and lunges purposefully at Smith.

Smith leaps back in alarm, raising his own sword. "Are you out of your fraking mind?!"

The words are hardly out of his mouth before Hatori again breaks into booming laughter, louder and more raucous than before. He is laughing so hard that he doubles over.

Then, just as suddenly he stops.

"Forgive me, Mr. Smith," he says with evident sincerity. "It was my duty to capture your attention."

Smith watches him bow, exit the platform, and disappear!

A sound from the bushes below the platform draws his attention and he looks down to see Greedley appear. "What the frak?" he yells.

Greedley smirks. "We've been waiting for this moment."

"Who's 'we'?" Smith demands.

The question is answered when a black-hooded figure emerges from behind the screen of vegetation and places a companionable arm around Greedley.

Who the frak is this? wonders Smith, staring down at them.

As the hood is pulled back, Smith recognizes his nemesis, Seraphim, Margaret's older sister!

Watching her stroke Greedley's hair makes him nauseous. *Yarrrgh!*

Seraphim can finance Greedley without blinking. And she's

obviously, if weirdly, deeply infatuated with him. No matter what I say, I'll never convince her that he's a bad guy!

Is this the end? Am I defeated already? He is stricken. Seraphim and J.P. have always disliked each other and feuded constantly. *But hurting my company is worse than any personal attack she has ever made against me!*

Without a word, he walks down the steps and turns away from the couple, moving down the path as quickly as he can. He hears laughter behind him but all he can think is, *How am I going to explain all this to Margaret?*

His shoulders slump as he makes his way back to the main building when out of nowhere Hatori appears beside him. As if nothing very remarkable has happened, they walk together, although Smith takes great pains to stay as far away from him as the path allows. With a vivid image of a menacing burning-eyed samurai, complete with bloodstained sword, he keeps an eagle eye on Hatori's hands.

"I must ask you, Mr. Smith," Hatori stops walking and bows again, "to please forgive me. I had no idea that Mr. Greedley and his companion intended any insult to you. When I realized that to my shame I had been used by them, I requested immediately that they leave the Kyoto Resort."

"That's good of you, Hatori San, but you didn't have to go that far," Smith tells him.

"In fact," Hatori says, "they are already packed and checked out. My security team is seeing to their departure as we speak."

He lowers his head again, but only slightly this time. "If you will accompany me?"

Smith keeps his mouth firmly shut. His brain in a hyper-alert state as he follows Hatori down a winding stone path, surrounded by mounds of moss-covered rocks and a variety of Japanese maples. A small stream runs beside it, expanding here and there to form a series of koi ponds. After walking for a while Smith bends over to examine the colorful fish and when he looks up, Hatori is gone. Disappeared. Again!

What the frak? For a moment he stands there in incomprehension, scratching his head. Then he realizes that what he's actually feeling is relief!

He decides to follow the path on his own, and soon comes to an iron gate. Beyond it, he can see a small but elegant traditional Japanese house.

A walkway of very fine gravel leads up to a set of three stairs, which Smith duly climbs. Observing several pairs of sandals in a row beside the door, he takes off his own shoes and lines them up neatly with the other footwear. He knocks on the wooden doorjamb. "Anyone here?"

A voice replies, "Please, enter!"

Immediately he recognizes Linc's voice, but he is utterly surprised to see Dame Georgina St. George standing beside her cousin. The disturbing events of the morning vanish in a bloom of elation and a huge smile stretches across his face.

Linc grins. "Are you finally ready to ride the tiger, Mr. Smith?"

He shakes his friend's hand. "You don't know how glad I am to see you both!"

He turns to Georgina. "How kind of you to be here. Believe me," he tells her earnestly, "I know now that I should have listened to you in the first place!"

"Sometimes," she replies enigmatically, " 'losing' can be winning if you learn from it."

"Yeah?" He is doubtful. "Maybe, but I'm disappointed in myself."

Linc shakes his head. "There's no time for that, Mr. Smith. Georgie has a great deal to teach you."

"Good, because I'm ready to learn! But, Linc, how do I explain all this to Margaret?"

The pro tilts his head to one side. "The first thing you might do is apologize, but I think that everyone is quite happy to be here. And," he shrugs, "Margaret has her own secret."

Distinct lines appear between Smith's brows. "What secret would that be?" he asks nervously.

"She had a feeling that the situation with her sister was not as it seemed," Georgina interjects. "It was Margaret who arranged for Linc and me to join your family outing. She might also be hoping for you to pull off a few miracles while we're here!"

"So," exclaims Smith, "Margaret knew everything all along! Well, from now on, I am ready to learn!"

"Good choice," the cousins reply in unison.

CHAPTER 3

ENERGY STATES

Who am I?

The next day J.P. and the family sit at their dining room table after lunch. "This place feels like a different planet," Margaret tells him with a soft chuckle.

"Does that mean you want to go home?" he asks, open, for now at least, to do anything she wants.

"Of course not, I had a fabulous spa treatment this morning. Two ladies poured warm herbal oil over my skin and massaged me for a very long time." She glances at her watch. "In fact, I have to run. I'm scheduled for another treatment in ten minutes."

"How much oil can they pour over you in one day?"

"Don't be silly. I'm having a music treatment this afternoon."

"Music?" he repeats, his brows rising in inquiry.

"Yes. The doctor told me that there are certain specific sounds which will help to balance my mind and body."

She pauses. "I wouldn't be surprised if you could benefit from a little music therapy, too." Looking at him fondly, she kisses his forehead. "You're a warrior, dear," she says, leaving the table.

A warrior, he thinks. *That doesn't sound bad. Not bad at all.*

With his butter knife, he masterfully mimes a golf swing in the air. He is about to get up when Georgina and Linc come over to his table and after a polite exchange, Georgina inquires, "Are you ready, Mr. Smith?"

"Oh, very," he replies.

She pulls a small computer out of her shoulder bag and opens it. "What I would like you to do now is take a short quiz."

He completes the quiz in minutes, signaling that he's finished.

"Good!" she says enthusiastically. "The results of this quiz will help you understand your Energy State, which will be extremely valuable for both communication and team building."

He then looks at his results and informs Georgina. "My results say that I'm a P Energy State person,"

"I'm not surprised, you have enormous energy and purpose, Mr. Smith, and you enjoy responsibility. You're a great doer and you're also a finisher! These are all qualities of a P Energy State person."

"Well, I guess I'm one of them."

"When you understand who you really are," she explains, "with all your tendencies, strengths and weaknesses, it will be much easier to deal with all the different situations that arise in business and in life. P Energy State individuals often make excellent leaders, as long as they stay in good balance."

"Is this a sort of personality test like the Myers-Briggs Type Indicator?" he asks. "We've used that at our company, and while it has limited value, it does help people understand each other better."

"The Energy State Quiz is far more than a personality test," she tells him. "Its origin lies in the Vedic health tradition of India known as Ayurveda. There is excellent research which shows, among other things, that your individual energy state or mind/body type can be correlated with the expression of certain genes in your individual DNA and with specific physiological measures. Ayurveda is even considered by some as an ancient science of epigenetics."

"Remind me, what is epigenetics?"

"Epigenetics," she explains, "is the science of how different environmental factors, such as diet and lifestyle, affect the expression of genes in the DNA, without changing its basic structure. Each of your trillions of cells has a DNA molecule that contains the totality of information needed to create and maintain your body. Within the DNA are genes, bits of information, which are constantly being turned on and off. Each time we learn a new habit, eat a new food, or encounter a new bacteria or virus, for example, certain genes react and adjust in harmony with each other to maintain balance in the physiology. Meditation, exercise, and virtually any new experience will alter gene expression.

"The real advantage of the Energy State Quiz as an assessment tool is that it identifies specific mental and physical factors that cause us to go out of balance and perform poorly. We are all different and react differently to environmental triggers. Understanding the specific nature of your employees, and what it is that affects them, makes it much easier to react to changes in the organization's environment so that everyone remains in balance and harmony.

"The three main Energy States in the quiz correspond to the three main brain/body types in Ayurveda. These have been traditionally referred to as Vata, Pitta, and Kapha. Since these words are largely unfamiliar to the West, we simplify the names and use only the first letter to identify them.

So," she goes on, "we call them V Energy State, P Energy State, and K Energy State. Sometimes we call them V, P, and K. In addition to these three simple Energy States, there are other combinations, such as VP Energy State or PK Energy State."

"Interesting," he says. "How do these states affect how people perform in business?"

"As a P Energy State person, Mr. Smith, you are goal-oriented, and your brain operates with a high degree of accuracy at medium speed. However, if you are not in balance you can become too intense and controlling, even irritable, and make mistakes in the heat of the moment."

He nods.

"On the other hand, a V Energy State person," Georgina continues, "has a brain that operates at a fast speed, processing information rapidly, but with a variable degree of accuracy. These people are creative whiz kids when they are well-balanced, but when they go out of balance they can become overly sensitive, nervous or anxious, or their attention may wander, and the result is that mistakes are made.

"In contrast to both P and V, a K Energy State person processes information more slowly but very thoroughly and accurately and can be a good administrator. When a K person is out of balance, he or she will have a tendency to become rigid and stubborn, which can result in poor performance and project delays."

Linc, who has been silent during the conversation, adds, "Perhaps a golf example would help?"

"Yes, please!" Smith responds enthusiastically.

Linc continues, "P golfers are very competitive, always looking at the flag and thinking about getting a par or better. But when they're out of balance, they become obsessed with small extraneous problems, like a sand trap or a water hazard."

"That's me, all right," admits Smith.

Linc nods, "A P Energy State person who is out of balance can even lose their temper if their ball goes into the water."

"I've seen that happen," Smith tells him. "I watched a guy hit three balls into the water and he got so mad that he threw all his clubs in!"

Georgina grins. "Some people like goals, while other people like procedures, and still others like options. We can make a general statement that goal-oriented people are predominantly P Energy individuals. K Energy State individuals prefer procedures, while predominately V Energy State individuals favor options."

Smith frowns. "What's an example from golf?"

"Okay," Linc says. "Why do you like to play golf, Mr. Smith?"

He shrugs, "Because I like getting low scores and winning. How is this different from a K person?"

"A pure K Energy State person," Linc tells him, "is more relaxed. They play golf because they enjoy having fun with friends.

They also take greater interest in the procedures of golf, like how to hit a draw or how to get out of a sand trap. They are even interested in the rules!"

"In business," Georgina explains, "K people are often administrators who like to examine every procedure and improve every process."

"So, what's the best thing to focus on?" Smith asks. "Goals, procedures, or options?"

"They're all good," Georgina tells him. "Focusing on goals is essential from the point of view of the leader. A marketing or sales person might want new options to get more customers. From another point of view, an administrator might want to focus on quality control and improve the current procedures before introducing any new ideas."

She laughs. "All of these qualities are necessary to improve a company. It's important to have clear goals, good procedures, and to be aware of, and open to, new options. It's ideal to have people with all three Energy States on each team. But no matter which type you may be, the really important thing is to stay in good balance.

"If a V person, for instance, goes out of balance, she or he might bring up too many options and disrupt the team coherence. On the other hand," she says, "if a K Energy State person becomes imbalanced, she or he can become stubborn and too focused on procedure and routine, which slows the whole team down. And if a P person is imbalanced, she or he can disrupt the entire team with their temper or their need to micromanage. Each of the three

Energy States has its own rhythm."

She chuckles, "I like to think of it as a 'Haiku rhythm.'"

"Oh, haiku!" says Smith. "Isn't that some kind of Japanese poetry?"

"You're familiar with Japanese poetry?" Georgina asks with mild incredulity.

"No," he says quickly, with an accompanying back and forth swipe of his hand. "I only know that they are incomprehensible to me!"

She laughs. "Haiku is the common word for 'hokku.' It's the opening verse of a form of Japanese poetry or linked verse. Haiku is a seed that contains the tree. It's small and simple, yet at the same time, it's large and meaningful. One of the most well-known examples of haiku is from Basho, the most famous haiku master of Japan." She holds up her index finger. "Bear in mind that there may be more than a hundred translations of this three-line poem:

> The old pond –
> A frog jumps in,
> And a splash.

The room is silent. Then Smith repeats, " 'Splash'? That's it? 'Splash'! I don't get where you're going with this!"

"Our inner rhythm," says Georgina as one hand slowly begins to move back and forth, "is like a haiku poem. It reveals who we are in life, everything we've ever been, as well as our future potential."

With a glance at his cousin, Linc interjects, "Can I demonstrate what you mean by this with a short golf lesson? Mr. Smith and I will go to the range for a few minutes."

"Excellent idea," she responds.

Smith feels as if he's just been rescued and needs no urging to follow his friend to the practice area.

Linc hands him a set of clubs and a bucket of balls and Smith hits them as hard as he can, imagining that each one has Greedley's face.

"Please remember, Mr. Smith," Linc tells him crisply, "I am absolutely unconcerned with how far your ball goes. What I do care about is that your swing is effortless!"

"Oh yeah," Smith says a little sheepishly. "I got it."

The pro explains, "It's important for you to check in with yourself and identify your inner rhythm. You went through a difficult experience with Greedley so it would be natural for your P Energy State to still be a little unbalanced today."

Smith nods in agreement.

Linc goes on, "When we lose our inner rhythm, it's impossible to have an effortless golf swing."

"You're right, that dang Greedley got me out of balance. Anything else I should watch for?" he asks.

"Think about what happens to you when you get overheated," suggests Linc.

Smith shrugs, "I took a Japanese bath just before lunch and almost boiled to death. I joined the men who were changing in and out of cotton robes in the dressing room. We sat on short wooden stools under a shower and scrubbed and shampooed every inch of our bodies. And these guys didn't just clean themselves once, but over and over again.

"The bath itself was beautiful, with a series of waterfalls at one end and adjoining private pools, but when I stepped into the scalding water I nearly screamed. One of the attendants must have noticed my body language because he asked if the water was too hot. I didn't want to look like a wimp, so I lied and said it was perfect!

"After soaking in there for what seemed like an insanely long time, but which was probably only a few minutes, I started to feel like a boiled lobster. In spite of my extremely relaxed muscles, I was freaking out."

"That's a good example," Linc tells him, "of a P person becoming disturbed when subjected to heat. I can't overstate how important it is for you not to get overheated, either mentally or physically.

"There is one more important environmental trigger," Linc points out, "which can aggravate your P Energy State."

"What's that?"

"Not eating on time!"

Smith laughs, "Boy, do I ever get hangry! And I can tell you that my family tries very hard to make sure that I eat on time."

"You must have a patient family, Mr. Smith. It's good that they have learned how to help you stay in balance. Your fire element is extremely strong. But just a few small tricks can really help a P Energy State person maintain their inner rhythm and stay balanced."

He adds, "Let me ask you something else. Can you remember how you felt when you were overheated and then ate your favorite ice cream, or took a cold shower?"

"Relief! I felt huge relief."

"Both cold and water are a P Energy State person's best friends," Linc tells him.

"Maybe, but I can't exactly jump in a lake while I'm at the office or playing golf."

"No, but you can keep wetting your head with cold water when the temperature is high, and make sure that you drink a lot of water—anything to keep you cool."

"Now that you mention it," Smith tells him, "I always find myself feeling better after a swim or a cold shower. And I like to keep the air-conditioning turned on high, which doesn't always suit my wife."

"Ah, yes, that can be a problem," Linc agrees. "There are times when different Energy States collide. And your wife's is different from yours. She took the quiz earlier and she is what we call a Tri-Energy State person, with an almost equal mixture of the three main Energy States. When they are in good balance, they give her the ability to adapt ideally to almost any situation. When Margaret is out of balance, she might be more sensitive to both heat and cold. Think about it, if Margaret really went out of balance, wouldn't your family life become more chaotic?"

"Absolutely! When I'm out of control, she keeps our life stable." He snorts, "With that Tri-Energy of hers, I've always thought she would make a good golfer!"

"That's probably true," agrees Linc, "but I think that she may have other things on her mind." He adds, "It's very good that you appreciate her strengths."

"I've always appreciated Margaret," Smith says fondly, "and I've always believed that she has a perfect temperament."

"You're a lucky man," Linc smiles.

"I sure am!"

Georgina is waiting for them when they walk back to the lodge. As soon as they are settled in some comfortable club chairs she asks, "What have you learned about the inner rhythm of your Energy State, Mr. Smith?"

He groans, "As usual, that I can be a hot head and that I need to keep my inner rhythm balanced."

"Each Energy State has its strengths and weaknesses. You benefit from your strengths when in balance, but when something in your environment causes you to become imbalanced, weaknesses show up."

"Power," adds Linc, "comes from effortlessness and from being in tune with your inner rhythm."

"In addition to discovering your Energy State," Georgina tells him, "there's a second tool I want to share with you. Total Brain Coaching starts with discovering your Energy State. The next tool is to create a Habit Map and Plan that will help change your habits."

"What kind of habits are you talking about?"

"Virtually every habit. For example, how do you feel about being on time?"

"I LOVE being on time. In fact, I might be at my most relaxed when I get to an appointment before everyone else. When I was a kid, my mom basically gave me two choices: Be on time or die."

"How do you feel when someone shows up late for a meeting?"

"I hate it, hate it, hate it, hate it. I have no use for late-comers!"

Repressing a smile, she continues, "So, would it be correct to say that much of your adult behavior towards others is shaped by habits learned when you were young?"

Before he has a chance to answer, she asks, "Is your wife always on time?"

He groans. "Never. I have to wait and wait and wait. It pretty much drives me crazy."

Georgina nods. "People with a predominantly P Energy State, like you, Mr. Smith, are goal-oriented and often have a strong need to be on time. But your wife has a Tri-Energy State. She has a different inner rhythm and different sense of time. Margaret is partially a K Energy State person, so being on time isn't as important to her. She's more relaxed about everything in life."

"That's Margaret all over!" he exclaims. "The crazy thing is that even when the clock shows that she's late, it usually turns out that there's been some sort of delay, maybe the person we are meeting is running late and her timing is perfect."

"I think we are done today," Georgina tells him. "Tomorrow you will learn how to be a samurai businessman."

"That sounds great. But, please," Smith begs, "no swords!"

"How can you be a samurai, Mr. Smith, without a sword?"

Energy State Quiz

The short quiz below, adapted from the book *Dharma Parenting*, gives you an idea of your Energy State.

V ENERGY STATE	STRONGLY DISAGREE / STRONGLY AGREE				
1. Light sleeper, difficulty falling asleep	[1]	[2]	[3]	[4]	[5]
2. Irregular appetite	[1]	[2]	[3]	[4]	[5]
3. Learns quickly but forgets quickly	[1]	[2]	[3]	[4]	[5]
4. Easily becomes overstimulated	[1]	[2]	[3]	[4]	[5]
5. Does not tolerate cold weather very well	[1]	[2]	[3]	[4]	[5]
6. A sprinter rather than a marathoner	[1]	[2]	[3]	[4]	[5]
7. Speech is energetic, with frequent changes in topic	[1]	[2]	[3]	[4]	[5]
8. Anxious and worried when under stress	[1]	[2]	[3]	[4]	[5]
V SCORE	(TOTAL YOUR RESPONSES)				

P Energy State	*Strongly Disagree* / *Strongly Agree*
1. Easily becomes overheated	[1] [2] [3] [4] [5]
2. Strong reaction when challenged	[1] [2] [3] [4] [5]
3. Uncomfortable when meals are delayed	[1] [2] [3] [4] [5]
4. Good at physical activity	[1] [2] [3] [4] [5]
5. Strong appetite	[1] [2] [3] [4] [5]
6. Good sleeper but may not need as much sleep as others	[1] [2] [3] [4] [5]
7. Clear and precise speech	[1] [2] [3] [4] [5]
8. Becomes irritable and/or angry under stress	[1] [2] [3] [4] [5]
P Score	*(Total your responses)*

K ENERGY STATE	STRONGLY DISAGREE / STRONGLY AGREE				
1. Slow eater	[1]	[2]	[3]	[4]	[5]
2. Falls asleep easily but wakes up slowly	[1]	[2]	[3]	[4]	[5]
3. Steady, stable temperament	[1]	[2]	[3]	[4]	[5]
4. Doesn't mind waiting to eat	[1]	[2]	[3]	[4]	[5]
5. Slow to learn but rarely forgets	[1]	[2]	[3]	[4]	[5]
6. Good physical strength and stamina	[1]	[2]	[3]	[4]	[5]
7. Speech may be slow and thoughtful	[1]	[2]	[3]	[4]	[5]
8. Possessive and stubborn under stress	[1]	[2]	[3]	[4]	[5]
K SCORE	*(TOTAL YOUR RESPONSES)*				

Compare your three scores. Whichever total is higher, V, P, or K, is your primary Energy State. It is common for people to have two high scores and one lower score. This indicates that you are a combination of two main Energy States, with a minor influence from the third one. In some cases, you may have three similar scores, which indicates that you have a Tri-Energy State. (Please note that this quiz can also be found in our book, *Total Brain Coaching*.)

CHAPTER 4

TOTAL BRAIN COACHING

A Personalized System for Habit Change

At precisely 9:00 AM, Smith is standing in front of Dame Georgina's hotel room door. He knocks but there's no answer except for explosive cries and guttural snarls.

Gingerly trying the door, he finds it open and peering inside, sees Georgina sitting with her knees tucked under her in front of a large screen. She is wearing a white open-neck yukata embroidered with small white birds.

The alarming sounds come from a video.

Patting the tatami mat beside her, she motions for Smith to sit. "Please," she says, "observe."

The video shows two Japanese warriors regarding each other warily, swords raised. Backlit by the rising sun, one man is ankle deep in the sea, while the other stands on the sand.

"The man on the beach is Sasaki Kojiro," Georgina tells him, "the best swordsman of his age. The other is Musashi!"

She looks expectantly at Smith. "You've heard of him?"

"No," he says.

Pausing the video, she explains, "Musashi was one of Japan's greatest warriors, a true samurai. The thing about Musashi," she says, waggling her index finger, "is that his swordsmanship was entirely effortless, perhaps because he put a great deal of effort into mastering it."

Then she pushes the play button and they watch the two samurai face each other. For long seconds the warriors stand immobile, gazing intently into each other's eyes. With small wary steps they inch first forward, then back, remaining in perfect balance like great cats with every sense alert.

This isn't like any sort of fencing Smith has ever seen. But up to then, his experience has been limited to corny Three Musketeer movies and Johnny Depp playing a saber-wielding pirate.

Both of these combatants, he notices, have two swords. One man holds a very long curved blade, which is drawn and raised, while the other has a short sword tucked into his belt. Without warning, they rush at each another—strike, parry, and jump back.

The camera zooms in for a close-up. Smith sees that Musashi has a gash in his forehead and blood is seeping through his russet brow band.

"Is that our guy?" he asks.

"Yes," Georgina says, "that is Musashi."

Why, he wonders, *does she want me to see the defeat of such an extraordinary warrior?*

Musashi's opponent has an almost tender expression as he sees blood drip slowly down Musashi's face. There is another shot of the loving glance of Kojiro, who—to Smith's complete surprise—sways slightly and collapses on the sand. Kojiro is dead.

The camera frames Musashi, who holds only the short sword in his hand, having thrown his larger weapon away. Musashi is the victor. Immediately, Japanese characters appear on the screen.

Smith suggests impulsively, "Let's see it again!"

Georgina starts the film again. "This time," she says, "bear in mind that Musashi's long sword is made entirely of wood."

"Wood?"

"Yes. His skill and inner confidence was at such a high level that he didn't need a long sword. Some biographers record that he didn't even use his short sword to dispatch Kojiro. Musashi killed his adversary with one blow from a wooden sword that he had carved from an old water soaked oar in the boat on his way to the match."

Watching more attentively this time, Smith is fascinated by the idea of such a perfect warrior. When the credits finish, Georgina turns off the video and looks closely at him.

"The actions of a master," she tells him, "arise from perfect balance and harmony. In order for us to achieve greatness, we must first be perfectly in tune with your own inner rhythm.

"Musashi wrote a famous book," she tells him, "which is still used by businessmen today, especially in Japan. It's called *The Book of Five Rings*."

Smith is curious.

"When we watch Musashi fight, it's impossible to see all his subtle movements. But they are the result of power and pure precision in brain and body.

The Way of strategy is the Way of nature. When you appreciate the power of nature, knowing the rhythm of any situation, you will be able to hit the enemy naturally and strike naturally.

"Musashi recognized that to be a true warrior, you must understand who you are and know your own inner rhythm.

"The first principle of Total Brain Coaching is knowing your Energy State, and the second principle is harnessing your neuroplasticity and your gut-brain axis. Neuroplasticity," she continues, "is the ability of the brain to change. When we do anything new—play a guitar, fly a plane, paint a watercolor, or bungee jump—it creates new connections in the brain. In fact, every single thing you experience changes your brain.

But Total Brain Coaching isn't only about the brain, it also includes detailed knowledge of the gut-brain axis and incorporates many time-tested recommendations on how to improve digestion and diet according to your individual Energy State.

"Your habits form neural circuits, which are strengthened by repetition. We learn to ride a bike when we are young and over time it becomes deeply embedded in the brain. Most people can still ride a bike even when they haven't done it for years.

"Think of a habit as a highway in your brain, over which information flows smoothly. With repetition it eventually becomes a super highway, which is difficult to remove. It's much easier and more effective for your brains to simply create a new road. Total Brain Coaching doesn't try to break old habits—it helps to create new ones."

"How is that accomplished?"

"We listen and ask certain questions so that each person can discover—for themselves—what habit they want to form and how they want to do it.

"This brings us to the third principle, the power of attention. There is a very wise old saying, 'Whatever you put your attention on grows strong.'

"As a Total Brain Coach your job is to help focus your client's attention on what needs to change. There are different ways that this can be done. Some coaches might use criticism and fear as motivation. This works in certain situations but it isn't sustainable or productive for long-term development and success.

"The quality of your attention as a coach is very important. It is vital to really listen to your clients to discover who they are, and how you can empower them to improve. Then you help them to create a plan to change their habits so that they can go on to become more successful."

She continues, "Another tool in Total Brain Coaching that we can take advantage of is finding your inner rhythm. A person in a V Energy State, for instance, moves very fast, while an individual in a K Energy State moves very slowly. By discovering the inner rhythm of your client, it is easier to help them form a new habit and integrate the new habit into their existing routines as effortlessly as possible."

Smith interrupts, "So, what you're saying is that as a P Energy State leader, I might push a K Energy State employee too hard."

"You're a fast learner, Mr. Smith."

"What are the other tools?"

"One of the most important tools is the feedback matrix."

"Whoa! I was just beginning to understand Total Brain Coaching. Now you're complicating it!"

"The feedback matrix might sound complicated but it's simply the principle of reinforcing the new habit through multiple feedback channels. We combine four different types of coaching: self-coaching, personal coaching, group coaching, and environmental coaching. We go into some detail about each of these in our workshops.

"The next principle of Total Brain Coaching is continuous improvement and integration, which I'm sure you are familiar with."

"Yes."

"One aspect of this tool is accountability. In order to make a real change, it helps to be able to measure it. If you want to adopt a new habit that could help you lose weight, for instance, you verify its effectiveness by getting on a scale once a week.

"The last principle is celebrate. At each stage, you give feedback that encourages and congratulates your clients—in your case, Mr. Smith, your employees—for every successful step in their habit change. Let your enthusiasm and drive become theirs."

"Great, I'm happy to start the Total Brain Coaching Workshops," he says "but will we have enough time?"

"I've just learned," she tells him, "that your sister-in-law's relationship with Greedley isn't going very well. Apparently, she's creating quite a commotion in his company."

He smiles knowingly.

"According to my sources, they have requested more time before submitting their final offer to Superflex. I would like to spend another day or two with you, going over these principles so that when you return to your company you will have the resources you need."

"I keep telling you, I'm too old to lead."

"I don't believe that and I don't think you do either," she says, every inch the Dame. "But you are still learning what it means to be a Musashi. You are familiar, Mr. Smith, with the phenomenon of athletes being 'in the zone'?"

"Of course, a lot of great golfers and basketball players have talked about it."

"The zone is a state where everything happens almost by itself and great feats are performed effortlessly. Each time Musashi fought," Georgina tells him, "he was in the zone. His mind and body were in a perfect state of balance and coordination. The athletes who speak about it often recount the experience of time slowing down and feeling that they are witnessing themselves making impossible actions.

"When you are operating in the zone, even in the midst of an overwhelming situation, nothing can overshadow it. You are naturally calm and aware, and spontaneously able to take advantage of a state of unlimited freedom and power.

"I am absolutely not advocating 'pretending' or making a mood of being in the zone," she tells him. "I'm talking about a real experience that comes from rewiring your brain so its powerful neural networks can make thousands of simultaneous computations.

Ordinarily, your small doubting self, located in the prefrontal cortex, interferes and casts crippling uncertainties. But when your brain is in a highly balanced state, there is no interference—we witness ourselves performing extraordinary movements. The small doubting mind is taken over by an integrated awareness, which is supported by a brain in which all parts are working coherently together."

She tells him, "There's a quote I like from the Zen fable *Neko no Myojutsu* or "*The Marvelous Techniques of the Old Cat*":

> As soon as there is the slightest conscious thought, however, contrivance and willfulness appear, and that separates you from the natural Way. You see yourself and others as separate entities, as opponents. If you ask me what technique I employ, the answer is mushin (no-mind). Mushin is to act in accordance with nature, nothing else.

Pointing to the far end of the room, Georgina asks, "Would you please hand me that golf ball?"

His eyes move to a new white golf ball sitting in the center of a low table and he gets up and tosses it to her.

In the split second that the ball is in the air, Georgina rises and draws a short sword from her yukata. She slices through the middle of the golf ball and re-sheaths the sword in one seamless motion!

He jerks his hand away. Oblivious to his bulging eyes and gaping mouth, Georgina leans over and calmly picks up the two perfect half-spheres of the golf ball.

Smith feels his heart pounding alarmingly in his chest. Worrying about his blood pressure, he follows her like a zombie, out of the room and out of building. Neither of them says a word, but as they continue to walk, he forces himself to breathe again and slowly begins to recover.

She explains, "We've heard that when a martial arts expert hits a piece of wood with his hand, he isn't thinking about hitting the wood itself, he's thinking of his hand going through the wood. Like everything in life, this movement should be effortless and fluid. Tension anywhere in the body or mind reduces your power.

"A master swordsman," she continues, "takes advantage of different tactics to win a battle, and he always controls the geometry of the space in which he fights. Attack and defense are simultaneous. Even on the defensive—new tactics can turn a defense into a surprise offense!"

Smith has an instant vision of himself outfitted head-to-toe as a samurai warrior.

"It is said," she recalls, "that Musashi once discerned the ability of a master swordsman by the way the man cut a flower with his sword."

"A flower?"

"Yes. It was a peony with a soft, supple stem. Musashi's power of observation lead him to determine, first, that the cut had not been made by a knife. Only a master warrior could make such a cut. When he tried to duplicate it with his own weapon, he could not make a precise cut that was nearly as clean or perfect. This told him that whoever had cut the peony was his superior in swordsmanship."

Smith shakes his head.

"Imagine," Georgina says, "that you are a samurai who is going to duel with a powerful enemy, one who you know is a better swordsman! Do you fight him or not?"

"I get it! You're telling me that I shouldn't have gone up against Greedley and Seraphim when I did."

"Exactly. If we have limited knowledge," she explains, "we can make poor choices."

"I've noticed," he says wryly.

"With your P Energy State, Mr. Smith, you are extremely sensitive to losing."

"No kidding!"

She laughs. "Nobody enjoys performing poorly, especially in front of others, but it's a real stress for a P Energy State person. This is the time for you to make a fresh start, learn more about Total Brain Coaching, and make a complete commitment, with no doubts, no second thoughts, as you begin to create coherence in your company. You must learn from the failures of the past and focus your attention and appreciation on success.

"I'll tell you a story that illustrates the importance of attention and appreciation. A good friend of Linc's, Kjell Enhager, helped coach the 1990 Swedish Women's golf team, who had been ranking about 20th in the world for a number of years. The first thing Kjell and the other coaches did was ask them what they considered a good score. One woman answered 'To shoot par.' And at that moment Kjell knew why their team wasn't #1."

Smith looks at her curiously. "Why?'

"In golf, at that time, everyone was aiming at par! Kjell and the other coaches had to change the team's mindset, so the first thing they had to do was to convince the members of the team that instead of reaching par, they would aim at getting a birdie on each hole. This would help them create the mindset, 'Everything is possible!' "

"But, how do you go about changing a person's mindset?"

"Good question. One of the things Kjell did was to ask the players a lot of questions that would produce a new way of looking at things."

"Like what?"

"For example, he asked if it was possible for them to make eighteen birdies in a row."

"And what did they say?"

"Everyone said no—because no one had done it yet! He also asked, 'How do you determine the number of shots you need to get a par three?' "

He jumps in, "That's easy, you reach the green in one shot, followed by two putts."

"That is exactly what the women said. But then," she continues, "he asked them, 'Who said that you need to have two putts?' "

Smith looks blank and Georgina chuckles, "None of the players were able to answer either. The fact is that if you are putting perfectly, you only need one putt on each hole."

"That's amazing!"

"Yes. The coaches wanted the team to accept that shooting a 54 was a real possibility."

He snorts, "That's sure a different mindset. Were they able to do it?"

"Not at first. No matter how hard they tried to think of it, or picture it, neither the players nor the other coaches could bring themselves to believe that it was possible."

"It is a bit of a stretch," Smith acknowledges.

"Maybe, but Kjell didn't give up. He asked if any of them had ever made a birdie on the first hole on their home course."

"I bet some of them had."

"All of the 28 women raised their hands," she tells him.

"That's impressive!"

"It is. And when he asked if they had ever made a birdie on the second hole of their home course, again, they raised their hands. Kjell went on to show them that since they had birdies on every hole during one round or another, it was, therefore, possible for them to get a 54 or better—all they needed to do was to get a birdie on every hole in the same round!"

"What did they think of this logic?"

"They accepted it completely and went on to become the #1 team in the world. And Annika Sörenstam, who was on the team, became one of greatest women golfers ever.

"Changing your mindset," she says, "will change your company and your life. You already know how easy it is to put your attention on mistakes made in your company and analyze every little thing you did wrong."

"Do I ever! Especially letting Greedley get the better of me."

"Kjell and his fellow coaches very strongly advised the Swedish team never to take that approach again. They told them to only focus on their best shots. Kjell said that they were to appreciate the details of how precise and perfect each one of those shots was!"

"I love this story!"

"After every meeting in your company, Mr. Smith, I want you to keep track of the good experiences and learn from the bad ones. Once you have grasped whatever there is to learn, maintain your focus on what works. Remember, every experience you have changes your brain."

"Every experience?" He is still skeptical.

"Every experience: stepping barefoot on a Lego, hearing a bird sing, smelling coffee. You may not be aware of the activity in your brain, but every single thing you see, hear, smell, taste, or touch, is changing it."

He shrugs, "What does this have to do with business?"

She responds patiently, "Your brain reacts to whatever you put your attention on. If you put your attention on your achievements, it reinforces the neural connections that support that action.

"I'm going to tell you about a list of questions Linc told the Swedish Women's golf team to ask themselves after every practice or round." She repeats from memory,

> What did I do well?
>
> What can I improve?
>
> How can I improve?
>
> What did I learn?
>
> What was FUN?"

He is quiet for a moment and then asks, "What if they didn't have any good shots?"

"If their answer was 'nothing,' Kjell would say, 'I understand that nothing felt really great today, but if anything was at all good, what would it be?' He also gave them a little notebook to record all of their progress.

"After three years, each member of the team had recorded over 1,000 positive memory deposits, and together, they listed a total of 28,000 deposits. Success breeds success," she tells him.

"Are you suggesting I use those same questions with my own employees in my company?"

"I suggest revising the questions slightly," she replies. "Have you ever read the book *Triggers* by Marshall Goldsmith?"

"No, I haven't."

"Goldsmith uses what he calls a daily spreadsheet that consists of a series of questions on how you are doing while you are trying to improve your life. Each question begin with the phrase, 'Did you do your best to….' For example, 'Did you do your best to practice your new habit today?'

"In his research he found that phrasing the question in this way made a huge difference in the person's ability to change! Some great coaches make a similar point, that winning isn't as important as giving 100%."

"Well, I don't know about that," he says. "I really like winning."

"If you like winning, then we have one more lesson today, which has to do with strategy. Have you ever had the opportunity to make the acquaintance of Sun Tzu?"

"Can't say I ever met the man."

She grins, "Sun Tzu was one of China's finest ancient philosophers. He is credited with writing *The Art of War*, a treatise on strategy, which has had profound influence on military thought throughout the ages. It's still applicable today in any contest of skill."

She pauses, "Businessmen love it."

"Okay, what does Sun Tzu say?"

"Sun Tzu realized that knowing yourself and your enemy, was essential for victory. Let me quote him as best I can."

> If you know the enemy and know yourself, you need not
> fear the result of a hundred battles. If you know yourself
> but not the enemy, then for every victory gained you
> will also suffer a defeat. If you know neither the enemy
> nor yourself, you will succumb in every battle.

"Yeah, but business," he grumbles, "isn't war!"

"Your opponents Greedley and Seraphim challenged you, Mr. Smith, but you weakened yourself."

"Whaat?"

"When you decided to confront Greedley, you were tired and you were out of balance. You were playing his game and not your own. If a business opponent resorts to unethical practice, you never want to lower yourself to his level. Focus, instead, on your own game! Greedley is also a P Energy State person, so it was in his nature to challenge and even taunt you. You must remember that you hold the advantage."

"I do? What is it?"

"You are starting to understand your own nature, your own inner rhythm. Two competing P Energy State individuals are like rogue elephants in the hot sun, but you know how to keep yourself balanced and play your own game.

"When you deeply understand each of the three Energy States," she tells him, "it becomes clear how the different types interact with each other. If you had been up against a pure K person, for instance, his slowness and habit of taking a long time to make a decision might have driven you crazy."

"I know that I can be impatient," he admits.

"The point is to know yourself and also know who your opponent is and what his or her strengths and weaknesses are."

"Ah, I'm starting to get it."

"It's ideal," she says, "if not vital, to create and maintain coherence in yourself and your company. You can behave aggressively, when you have full information and when you can be spontaneously in tune with your inner rhythm."

He heaves a sigh. "I know I made a mess of meeting Greedley and Seraphim. I was humiliated."

"One of the most important concepts in Total Brain Coaching, as we've said, is to learn from your failure. A great warrior often has to fail before he can finally achieve victory."

Smith frowns. "I remember something like that happening in an old movie about a Shogun, some machismo dude with a name that sounds like Toyota."

"Ah yes, Toranaga! The character of Toranaga is loosely based on the life of a real Shogun, Tokugawa Ieyasu, a powerful leader who was a serious student of the art of war."

"Margaret is always telling me to pick my battles!"

The path curves as they walk under the shade of tall coconut palms. Giant ferns grow on the side of the mountain and at one point Smith feels the cooling spray of a shower of foaming white water from volcanic rock high above them.

"You were only lacking the knowledge of Total Brain Coaching," Georgina reassures him. "Even at this early stage, you are well on your way to becoming a Shogun."

Smith likes the sound of that.

CHAPTER 5

THE ZEN GARDEN

The Way of the Warrior

The next day Georgina picks Mr. Smith up in the golf cart and drives him to the far end of the resort. Stopping the cart beside yet another Japanese cottage, she tells him that she has brought him here to show him a garden.

"A garden?" He looks at her in surprise. "Okay, but it's a shame we didn't bring my wife. Margaret loves gardens."

"This is a different kind of garden, Mr. Smith," she says, leading him into the little house.

"All the more reason to bring her," he responds, following her through a large circular opening to an open porch.

"You're very welcome to bring Margaret here, if you'd like," Georgina says warmly, "but today's visit is part of your introduction to Total Brain Coaching."

A pair of wide double doors lead into a main room which is almost completely open on the far side. The consultant gestures towards a bench facing a flat expanse of carefully raked white sand.

Smith sits down on the bench. *Where*, he wonders, *is the garden?*

All he can see is sand and a few large upright rocks that look as if they were placed at random. Some of the rocks lie flat. There are also three large gnarled and evidently ancient bonsai trees, but…no flowers. Staring at the scene before him, he realizes for the first time that one of his lifelong assumptions has always been: *No flowers, no garden.*

"Please," Georgina gestures around them, "enjoy!"

With his mouth pressed into a thin line, he stares at the rocks and the raked sand for several minutes. "Uh, Georgina," he says at last, "where's the garden?"

"This," she gestures to the sandscape before them, "is a Zen garden!"

His face is blank.

"It's a copy," she explains, "of one of the most famous Zen gardens in Kyoto. As you see, it's the shape of a rectangle."

"Yes, I see."

She continues, "The rectangle encloses five groups of fifteen stones, each of a different size. Every day at dawn, the head gardener, who was once a Zen monk, carefully rakes the fine white gravel. Such a garden is meant to be viewed from the veranda of a monastery, a setting the resort has tried to replicate for their guests."

He struggles for words—"Don't you find it…kind of…bland?"

"I understand," she concedes, "why this might appear to be true, Mr. Smith. But if you can be very still for a while and allow your physiology to become settled and balanced while you are viewing, you may have a different experience. To the ancients, these gardens represented lakes and plains and mountains, the great mysteries of nature which hold the meaning of life. Maybe think of it that way."

After some minutes he sighs, "I just don't see it. Don't get me wrong, Georgina, bonsai trees are great. But to me, this so-called 'garden' looks like the far side of the moon."

"Have you ever noticed that some golf courses, especially around the greens, have a Japanese influenced design? The point of the Zen garden is to help calm your mind, open your senses, and expand your awareness. There is a lot of research that shows that the brain is affected by many different things. When we see virtually anything, it causes some part of our brain to become active, and when we smell something, another part becomes activated. The same goes for hearing, taste, and touch. Different Energy States people also react differently to sensory information. For example, a P or K person may have a high pain threshold, while a V person will likely have a much lower threshold. The point is that Total Brain Coaching expands all of the senses in each Energy State to create greater balance in the mind and body, and this allows greater awareness.

"Most businesspeople," she tells him, "have been educated in what we might think of as an 'old school' style of mental and physical training, and the result is that their minds and bodies are deeply stressed from a young age. Their ego and their intellect dominate their lives, and their self-esteem depends almost entirely upon the approval of others. It's very rare that such people are able to realize their full potential."

She turns to face him. "Musashi had his own code to help him evolve."

He's suddenly interested. "What was that?"

"He called it the Way of the Warrior, but it was different from the samurai's traditional code of Bushido. His second book, *The Way of Walking Alone*, which he wrote right before his death, includes 21 precepts of his personal code, such as, 'Accept everything just the way it is; Think lightly of yourself and deeply of the world; Never stray from the Way.' In both books, Musashi explained that he always wanted to challenge himself, to break the boundaries of the world he was living in and go beyond them."

Smith pauses. "But wasn't he taking a big chance in every encounter?"

"He certainly was. At that time, there were no winners or losers in sword fighting, only survivors. If you lost, you were dead or permanently injured," she says soberly. "Worse than that, you were dishonored for the rest of your life."

"High stakes!"

She explains, "He felt that if he were up against a better opponent he would be challenged to rise to more refined levels of creativity and action. He appreciated his opponent's style of fighting, but he himself was not educated in the specialties of the various schools of swordsmanship. Musashi was what we might call a 'gut player,' who repeatedly placed himself in situations that forced him to learn by going beyond his immediate skill level. He started as a samurai, but when his master died he became a ronin, a wandering warrior."

"I hope you're not suggesting that I adapt that type of action in my business practices?"

She chuckles, shaking her head. "No, what I'm saying is that Musashi would only challenge an opponent when he had complete confidence in himself and in his own skills. When you achieve 100% confidence in your abilities, 100% of the time, it's only natural for you to want to go beyond and test yourself. Musashi did not fight more skilled swordsmen in order to glorify his reputation or to gain wealth or power. He fought because his greatest desire in life was to transcend the limitations imposed by his small ego. He wanted to live fully in the present and he risked his life to experience a state of unimaginable power and freedom and bliss."

Smith's hand shoots up. "Waaait a minute. I value everything I've learned from you, Georgina, and I've learned a lot, but I didn't sign up for a life or death experience."

"Of course not. Business is a more compassionate occupation than sword fighting!" she grins. "And losing doesn't have the same consequences!

"Musashi's art required complete commitment on every level. Not only was he involving himself in a life or death situation, it was his deepest desire to attain the ultimate level of reality—to personally realize the unbounded unified field of all the laws of nature—in other words, to become enlightened. Swordsmanship was a doorway Musashi used to expand his inner awareness and empower and refine his life."

"Is that all he did, sword fighting?"

"Musashi was also a master calligrapher, painter, and sculptor.

He equated his understanding of swordsmanship with his style of calligraphy. There are some insightful articles about Musashi, and one of them, entitled *The Brush is the Sword of the Mind* includes samples of his calligraphy."

She continues, "If anyone—a businessperson, warrior, scholar, priest, or even the simplest man or woman—can go beyond the boundaries of ordinary life and have a clear experience of their inner self, which is their own true nature, even for a short time, then all their behavior, all their action, spontaneously becomes in tune with nature. The experience of this state on a permanent basis is traditionally described as the state of enlightenment."

"So, should I visualize myself being enlightened?" he asks. "When I'm doing something, for instance, should I hold some particular thought or affirmation?"

"Absolutely not!"

He has never heard her speak so forcefully and is slightly taken aback.

"To make a pretense or a mood of enlightenment," she explains, "actually produces a negative effect on both your body and mind. If you are living in a shack, but you repeat, 'I live in a palace', over and over again, it won't create the reality of a palace, but it will divide your mind and create a state of cognitive dissonance, or internal confusion. You really are living in a shack and experiencing all that this entails, while at the same time you are pretending, on the level of the intellect, to be living in entirely different circumstances."

Smith is confused. "What about 'positive affirmations'? "

"Used correctly, positive affirmations have value. In this case, however, what is going on is self-delusion, which has an adverse affect both on your psychology and on your behavior. In order for enlightenment to be real, it has to be natural and spontaneous."

"I wish," Smith says wistfully, "I knew a real Musashi."

"You can be a real Musashi!" Georgina tells him. "One of his great secrets was that he did a lot of meditation."

"How can a warrior also be a meditator? It seems like a contradiction."

"Historically, meditation was complementary to the mastery of the martial arts. Even today, it's the most powerful tool for preparing for action, any action, because meditation cultures a state of perfect mind-body coordination. The finest martial experts have often spoken and written of feeling the energy of the universe flowing through them, and their breath becoming the breath of the cosmos.

"Our ego and intellect can criticize and undermine our confidence and performance. Toxic dialogue such as: 'I'm never going to make it,' or 'I don't think I'm good enough,' or 'I'm going to blow it in front of everybody!' is negative thinking about events that haven't yet come to pass and which might never occur. By putting our attention on them, we are creating in ourselves a mental and physical state which can only result in poor performance. We are reinforcing defeat in our brain."

"I have had many nagging doubts," Smith agrees.

"The purpose of meditation," Georgina tells him, "is to allow you to experience your true nature. The nervous system is gradually able to unfold its full potential, and with practice, you increasingly enter into 'the zone' during activity."

"Hey, I want to be in the zone too," he protests. "I just don't want to risk my life to do it."

"Of course," she agrees. "Musashi reached this state through an activity that was dangerous and exceedingly challenging indeed, and I don't recommend that you take up swordsmanship!

"However, if we prepare properly, then during a high level of challenge, it's not uncommon to suddenly find ourselves 'in the zone' even for a few moments. Because of long-term fatigue and stress in our nervous system, unfortunately this doesn't happen all the time."

"Stress is a part of living," Smith says. "I don't see how it can be avoided."

"That's very true and because we can't always control our external environment, even at home, we need a process or technique that allows us to regularly culture this state ourselves. If more people had access to such a technique, they would experience being in the zone more frequently. Eventually, this powerful state would be available to them, not only in highly challenging situations, but every moment of their life."

"I guess Musashi was a warrior in the best sense of the word," he says thoughtfully, "but I'm not sure his stoic lifestyle would fit into today's world. I mean, it was pretty extreme. Don't you think?"

She laughs, "I'm also not advocating Musashi's lifestyle. The haiku master Basho said,

> Do not seek to follow in the footsteps of the wise. Seek what they sought.

"For thousands and thousands of years," she explains, "extreme methods have been used to attempt to reach this state. Many people became monks, living in caves and spending hours and years in silent contemplation or concentration. Others sought transcendence in activity, but the aim was the same—to experience a state of perfection and freedom, a state of simply being."

Smith imagines himself, sitting in a frigid cave in the Himalayas, trying to improve his business performance!

"Fortunately," she says, "the most effective approach is one which has been followed by warriors for thousands of years all over the Far East, especially in India. Buddhism, you may know, originated in India, and later spread to other countries. One of the most profound treatises on meditation and enlightenment ever written is the *Bhagavad Gita*, from the Vedic tradition of India. This remarkable document recounts a conversation between a noble warrior and his fully enlightened teacher on the battlefield."

She pauses. "I'm sure you've seen the golf movie, *The Legend of Bagger Vance*?"

"Sure, I see every movie that has golf in it."

"This particular golf movie is based on the *Bhagavad Gita*, though they don't say anything about meditation."

"Whenever you mention meditation," Smith tells her, "I can't help but think about weird postures, or lying on a bed of nails, or contemplating my navel."

He adds, "You gotta know, Georgina, I'm not the kind of guy who concentrates on nothingness!"

She laughs gently. "The technique I recommend for you involves absolutely no contemplation or concentration. It simply makes use of the natural tendency of the mind to go to a field of greater and greater happiness. It's relaxing and easy to learn."

She pauses, looking at him. "But you really don't remember Linc recommending it to you years ago as the supreme technique for golf mastery?"

"Oh, yeah, yeah, yeah," he says uncomfortably. "I suppose I remember. But I just never got around to it. I mean, if all you want me to do is to relax, lying in a hammock or listening to music seems a lot easier."

"Funnily enough, it's really not easier," she tells him. "It would be a great misunderstanding to think of this particular form of meditation as mere relaxation. This practice is a dynamic process of going within and naturally expanding your creative intelligence."

"That sounds great and I meant to learn it. I even came close a few times. But isn't it possible to get a little too relaxed and laid back in our fast-paced competitive society?"

"Some of the most active and successful businessmen in the world practice this form of meditation," she tells him.

"We can continue this conversation at another time, but as your coach and mentor, it's my responsibility to offer you the fastest, most reliable, natural, and thorough procedure to become a samurai."

Walking back to the clubhouse, Smith thinks about what she just said. When he gets to the main lobby, he is again drawn to the ancient ink sketch. But this time, instead of rushing past, as he's done every day since he arrived, he stops to examine it closely.

An appealing old monk sits with his legs folded beneath him. His eyes are closed and there's a beatific expression on his face. On the wall beside the artwork, an engraved bronze plaque bears the name, Miyamoto Musashi.

CHAPTER 6

MORE COHERENT COMMUNICATION

Balancing Your Energy State to Improve Communication

Memo: April 9
From: J.P. Smith
To: Executive Team

1. Meeting 4:00 PM today

2. Important news about Greedley

Doug Hatchett, CEO, Ben Arnold, President, and Anne Bright, chief legal counsel, are already in the conference room. As Smith enters, he notices that Hamilton Jr. is sitting next to Georgina at the far end of the table.

Odd for him to attend an executive meeting, but, he thinks, *she must have invited him.*

He opens the session by describing his encounter with Greedley and Seraphim in Kauai. Then he talks about his training with Georgina and his decision to resume personal control of the company, quickly reassuring Hatchett that the move is only temporary.

Although visibly disturbed, Hatchett is nevertheless able to curb his temper and describes a new plan to substantially sweeten their offer to Superflex.

"What do you think?" Smith asks the others.

"I'm not sure that our credit is good enough to borrow such an amount," Anne tells him. "How are we going to pay it back?" Ms. Bright, an adept and experienced lawyer in her early fifties, holds a conservative outlook on life, especially in business, and her thoughtful cautious nature has often been a valuable counterpart to Smith's more impulsive executives.

"Even if the purchase of Superflex boosts sales," she says with sincere concern, "the debt involved is just too big. It makes us even more vulnerable to a takeover."

Hatchett leaps to his feet. "Takeover! Are you crazy?"

Calmly, she points out, "We have a responsibility to avoid placing the company at risk."

"Last week," he says, "you were all over a strategic management plan and now you're being mealy-mouthed!"

"Conditions," she says, pausing, "have changed."

Hatchett wheels around to face Smith. "We need to up our offer immediately and get control of those great new sports technologies. It's do-or-die!"

Smith asks Ben Arnold for his opinion, but before he can respond Hatchett cuts in. "Anything he has to say is going to be colored by his relationship with Greedley. The two of them talk all the time."

Smith turns to Ben. "Is this true?"

Ben, glares at Hatchett. "It certainly isn't. I don't know what he's getting at, but he better watch himself!"

"You spoke to Greedley yesterday," accuses Hatchett. "I heard your assistant say that he was on the phone."

"Are you in contact with Greedley, Ben?" Smith asks.

"I have some personal business with Greedley, J.P., which, I promise you, has nothing to do with the company."

A long silence follows broken by Anne. "We would be able to negotiate better if we could find out what Superflex wants."

Hatchett, Smith observes, *looks like he wants to jump over the table and cleave Anne's skull with his namesake weapon!*

"The issue at stake," says Hatchett, "is money!"

Smith turns to his star consultant. "Any thoughts, Georgina?"

"Mr. Hatchett deserves great credit for his determination to do whatever is needed in a timely fashion," she responds. "And Ms. Bright has made some very good points on the risks involved as well as another approach to negotiating."

She pauses a moment. "Let me change the topic briefly and ask if all of you have had a chance to take the Energy State Quiz?"

Smith isn't sure where she's going with this, but a distraction at this point can only improve things.

"Yes," Hatchett replies, obviously still frustrated and angry. "I did the damn quiz!"

"Really? What did you learn about your own Energy State?" she asks interestedly.

"I learned that I'm a P Energy State person, whatever that means."

Georgina turns to Ms. Bright. "How about you, Anne?"

"I appear to be a K Energy State individual," the lawyer replies.

"And you, Hamilton?" asks Georgina.

"The quiz results indicate that I have all three Energy States in equal amounts," he tells her. "Is that okay?"

"Yes," she says, "It is called a Tri-Energy State. It is an unusual but powerful combination when it's in good balance."

"What's your Energy State, Mr. Arnold?" she asks.

"I appear to be a combination of P and K."

Hatchett interrupts, "What are these Energy States anyway and what do they have to do with our present crisis?"

"I know that you are concerned about improving our offer to Superflex, Mr. Hatchett. But Greedley hasn't finalized his offer yet so we have to wait and find out what we are up against. In the meantime, there is a lot we can do to improve the performance and success of this company and Mr. Smith and I have discussed some new ideas. The first step," she tells him, "is to have everyone in the company take the Energy States assessment quiz. This simple tool will help improve communication within the company."

"What's wrong with our communication?" Hatchett demands.

Ignoring his comment, Smith suggests, "Perhaps, Georgina, you could start by telling us more about the Energy States."

She then gives a short introduction to each of the Energy States, explaining their strengths and weaknesses.

"Could you tell me more about having three Energy States?" asks Hamilton Jr.

She looks at him, "As a combination of Energy States, your V gives you an inquiring and creative mind, your P gives you a sharp intellect, while your K gives you a steady and friendly nature."

Hamilton beams. In contrast, Smith notices that Hatchett's face is almost purple with impatience.

"I don't see how any of this is going to help," he bursts out.

"It's getting a little late," Georgina concludes. "Why don't we continue this discussion tomorrow with a fresh mind."

Not a moment too soon, thinks Smith.

"Dame Georgina is right," he announces, "it's getting late. My assistant will notify you when we will meet again to discuss a new course of action. This meeting is officially adjourned."

Hatchett stands up, knocking his chair over behind him before storming out of the room. Hamilton exits the scene with the stride of young warrior. He is experiencing a very minor victory, but a victory nevertheless.

When everyone but Georgina has gone, Smith releases a sigh of relief. "It got a little hot in here, don't you think? I must say, Georgina, it was shrewd of you to compliment Hatchett."

"Unfortunately," she says, "in his eagerness to be right, he neglected an important principle."

"What's that?"

"Respecting other people's feelings. It accomplishes nothing to be right if you upset someone's feelings so much that they either cannot grasp what you are trying to communicate, or they simply stop listening. Building coherent management requires clear, smooth lines of communication, and right now this is missing from your top level management."

"You're right," Smith exclaims. "Our meeting was like a family feud."

She smiles ruefully. "Hatchett got his message of urgency across, but at the expense of injuring Anne's feelings and creating dissension and disharmony in the group."

"Well, this is a place of business," he replies defensively, "not a kindergarten."

"Of course, but what we witnessed here happens all the time, not only in business, but at home, in school, and in kindergarten as well. One of the keys to Total Brain Coaching is to make sure that each individual is well-rested and in good balance. Mr. Hatchett has quite a temper."

"That's putting it mildly."

"P Energy State people tend to become angry when they go out of balance and it takes only a simple trigger to cause this. For example, I bet anything that Hatchett missed lunch today!"

She continues, "Understanding his own Energy State, with its strengths and its weaknesses, will help him to better manage his temper. That alone will help everyone he interacts with, and, therefore, also help the company. Unless he improves his ability to listen and communicate, there isn't much hope to create a coherent team."

Smith nods reluctantly.

"It is your task as a leader and manager, Mr. Smith, to redirect the flow of energy of your team members towards higher and more useful goals than fighting among themselves. Coherent communication is like a fine cord that binds together all of the elements necessary to build a coherent management team. The degree of cooperation, commitment, and inspiration in any group depends upon the manager's ability to facilitate communication. Essentially, a Total Brain Coach or manager does one primary thing."

"What's that?"

"He or she shapes the flow of attention of the employees. And how this is accomplished can vary dramatically, depending on the situation. The quality of coherent communication that takes place during any exchange between employees is a critical benchmark of a manager's success. Whatever else may be going on, it's important to have your attention on facilitating successful communication at every level, and constantly ensure that the flow of communication is smooth.

"There are, of course, different levels of communication. The most obvious is on the level of the mind and the most hidden and powerful is on the level of emotions. If someone's feelings are hurt, it will immediately create an imbalance in their minds and actually impede their intellectual decisions. This isn't always obvious since most of us have learned to hide our emotions, even from ourselves. Coherent communication means understanding and reacting appropriately to the subtleties of each other's Energy State."

"I'm curious," Smith says, changing the subject, "why did you included Hamilton at the meeting? He barely has his MBA and he's working for Westport Consulting."

"You are right, but I would like to have him join SMITH & HATHAWAY and for the time being act as my assistant, if you don't mind. I know that he's still young and naïve, but I believe he has great potential."

"I don't have a problem with that, since he's the son of one of my main stockholders, " he replies. "I need to say, Georgina, that even though Hatchett went overboard criticizing, I still think he has the company's interest at heart."

"Overboard," she says, "is the key word here. Coherent communication takes the feelings of others into account. It is important to be able to be open and have different opinions. A lively discussion and debate is a very good way to exchange ideas and reach a consensus. What we want to avoid is unnecessarily becoming angry and damaging another person's feelings. If communications can create harmony on the level of the feelings, it strengthens the overall coherence of the company, and the company will begin to exhibit a wholeness which far exceeds the sum of the parts."

"Oh, come on, Georgina, everyone has their feelings hurt occasionally. We're grownups. What's the big deal?"

"It's a big deal because it destroys coherence. The conflict between Hatchett and Anne must stop," she states. "Even though I believe that Ms. Bright may be capable of protecting herself, she's still vulnerable to his attacks. Because of her K Energy State she tends to speak more slowly and is more careful in making decisions. This is a very valuable asset in an individual responsible for the legal obligations of a company. Anne is even-tempered and stable, but Mr. Hatchett's constant assaults will eventually undermine her good nature and upset her emotions. These two should be working together and use their energy to find a creative solution to the company's problems."

"I'm not a psychiatrist, y'know," he protests.

She chuckles. "You're not, but being a good manager," she says, "is very much like being a good father or a good coach. A coach helps resolve such situations by acting as a third party, empathizing with and supporting both sides. He isn't concerned with who is right or wrong, only clarifying and resolving the issues at hand. The simple act of bringing your personal attention to the situation has the effect of helping to create harmony and better feelings.

"See if you can get Mr. Hatchett to be more considerate of Anne's feelings in the future. Remind him that she is a very valuable member of the company. At the same time, try to get Anne to be aware that even though Hatchett may have a weakness when interacting with people, he's also an experienced executive."

"What if Hatchett wants me to back him against Anne?"

"If Hatchett or anyone else tries to bring up the issue of who's right and who's wrong, you need to bring their attention back to the larger objective of trying to save the company. Inspiration is key. The ultimate task of a good manager is to offer his employees such a high level of inspiration that they forget their differences for the good of the company. Each employee has to feel part of a bigger whole, a bigger team."

"But how long does the inspiration last? Sooner or later, won't they just go at each other again?"

"Bonds are created when people are inspired to think in higher terms, and when an ideal is shared," Georgina tells him.

"But can people really change their attitudes?" he asks.

"Ideal communication produces a state of coherence, which results in fewer mistakes and higher achievement."

"Okay," he says, "You're telling me that communication is an important factor in generating an optimal team. I accept that, but I think there could be a lot of resistance if I start telling everyone to tiptoe around each other's feelings."

"You are only asking certain people to change their habit of poor communication. In the next few days we will set up some Total Brain Coaching Workshops," she tells him, "and the principles of the Coherence Code will be presented to your employees. A leader creates coherence by communicating the missions and goals of the company and by inspiring all of the managers and employees to go beyond themselves. This is what you are going to do with your employees."

He's silent for a moment, then he says, "I have an idea. How about you make the inspirational speech for me?"

"No," she shakes her head slowly. "It's got to be you, Mr. Smith. You have to fill your employees with inspiration, trust, and support. And you have to do it over and over again as you gradually rebuild confidence. I know you'll do a great job! I have an appointment tomorrow, otherwise I would be there with you. Can you come to my office in Connecticut this weekend and give me a report?"

"Of course."

There's a knock on the door. His assistant opens it a crack and peeks in. "Mr. Smith?"

"Yes?"

"There's a message for Dame Georgina."

"Who is it from this time?" he responds impatiently.

"It's the attaché to the Secretary General of the UN," she says. "He wants to remind her that she is addressing the General Assembly tomorrow morning."

CHAPTER 7

TOTAL BRAIN TEAM COACHING

Habit Change to Improve Teamwork

Memo: April 11
From: J.P. Smith
To: Georgina

1. How to deal with Hatchett disapproval of my taking over as president

2. How much time do we have before Greedley makes his final offer

On Saturday afternoon Smith is standing in front of a two-story sandstone building surrounded by 24 wooded acres. Why would Georgina have an office in Connecticut when she does business in New York? The place looks more like an elegant home than a place of work!

He raps his knuckles against the wide oak door, which opens promptly. A short very British young man introduces himself as Georgina's assistant and ushers him into the building, escorting him down a hall and through French doors into a beautifully landscaped courtyard.

Politely suggesting that he take a seat on one of several

ergonomically curved chairs beside an exquisitely carved marble fountain, the assistant leaves Smith to enjoy the late day peaceful atmosphere. Birdsong fills the air as he looks around him at the tall trees and flowering plants.

He puts one hand up to cover a yawn and then another. *Maybe, he thinks, yawning again, I'm relaxing.* Closing his eyes for a moment, he leans back and begins to doze off.

Three-quarters of an hour later he wakes to hear Georgina calling his name. Leaning out of an open window on the opposite side of the courtyard, she is waving at him and pointing to an open door.

Smith inhales a fragrant scent in the air. *Sandalwood maybe? Hah, a management consultant's office that smells of sandalwood!*

He enters a high-ceilinged room, its walls hung with paintings. *That's the kind of art that looks like it should be in a museum, but here it is, in front of me!*

Georgina offers him a seat on a comfortable couch facing a cabinet of inlaid wood. The coffee table in front of him holds a silver tray with two good-size china mugs, a steaming pitcher of milk, and a plate piled high with what look like homemade cookies.

She extends her hand invitingly, "Please."

He stares at the hot milk. *I guess there's a first time for everything,* he thinks, reaching for it.

He takes a small, cautionary sip and discovers that the drink is quite good! It has a delicate flavor, which he can't identify, but which he thinks he could easily become addicted to. The taste is remarkably delicious.

"I'm very glad you could come," Georgina tells him. "How did your speech go yesterday?"

"Terrific." He bites into a pecan nut cookie. "I put fire into my people!"

"Very good," she laughs.

"At the end of the meeting, a few of the boys in the mailroom even came over to say that they would buy stock if it would help. On what they earn, they couldn't afford many shares and I appreciate their offer. I tried to be honest with them, and told them that I knew that there were problems in the company and from now on no one will be pressured into recommending any product they don't believe in.

"I said that we are going to set an example and show the world that even today, values go hand in hand with success. They must have thought that I was serious because they started to applaud."

"It appears that you have a team, Mr. Smith!"

"Yeah," he agrees. "But Hatchett is furious with me for taking over again."

"Change can be difficult at first. You need to watch him carefully and try to soothe his feelings. It's not going to be easy. And as soon as possible, begin Total Brain Coaching Workshops so that your managers can create more productive teams!"

"Just how does Total Brain Coaching apply to teams?"

"Like individuals, teams can have bad habits," she points out. "As a Total Brain Coach, it's up to you to help them discover what their bad habits are so that you can then help them to identify better ones."

"Such as?"

"At this point you have several very dysfunctional teams with managers who are still using the command and control method of business management—telling the team members what to do rather than listening to them and empowering them. This top-down style will unfortunately not reinforce their habits to become innovative and meet customers' needs quickly."

"But I built SMITH & HATHAWAY by making sure that everything was done correctly. And I chose my senior staff based on their ability to give clear, specific orders so that everyone does what they were supposed to."

"That may have worked in the past, but we live in a high-tech age which is driven by constant change. It's time to make a change and improve the habits and mindset of your company."

She looks at him calmly. "Let me ask you a simple question. If you could wish for one thing for your company, what would it be?"

He answers immediately, "A boatload of money."

"Since that's not on the table right now, does anything else come to mind?"

"After my talk, I asked the group what improvements they thought would help the company. There were a few suggestions, but most importantly I was listening to them and they knew that I really cared. I think what's missing in our company is trust."

"Yet you asked for their ideas. That is a great first step in creating a new mindset of trust in your employees."

"So, all I have to do is install a big suggestion box and everything will be fine?"

"What is it that you think you need to do?"

He sighs, narrowing his eyes. "I guess you're right. I have to look for ways to change our current corporate mindset. And I know that begins with me. My worst habit is that I like to micromanage, which isn't a good way to create trust."

"Okay, let's begin with you. What habit would you like to change in your own behavior?"

"There's a long list, but if I were to start with something practical it would be how I conduct myself at executive meetings. I used to be very controlling and I don't want to be like that any longer. I also used to interrupt people and force my ideas on them. I want to listen more and delegate more!"

"Good choices, which lead us to the creation of a Habit Map and Plan."

They spend the next half hour working on it with the result that Smith decides to start with the simple habit of listening more right away. He would try to be silent for most of his meetings, and only give his opinion at the end. He would also do a daily check-in with Georgina for the first week.

"But, how is changing one habit going to save my company?"

"It won't," she says simply. "But it will set an example and encourage the others to change their own habits. Simultaneously, you need to encourage each team to change their habits so that they can be in line with the company's goals, and also more effective. It is going to take time, Mr. Smith. Change begins within and you have taken the first and most important step in the process by starting to change your own habits.

"I hope you won't mind," she adds. "I asked Hamilton Jr. to stop by for a few minutes to give you an idea of how the Total Brain Coaching Workshops fit into the most current theories of management. He has some interesting ideas for the future of your company."

"You must be kidding," Smith says, then he pauses and nods his head, "Oh, I get it. You're trying to please his father, right?"

"For the moment, let's not concern ourselves with my reasons," she tells him. "Let's just hear what he has to say."

He smiles as if to say that he understands and Georgina presses a button on a small ivory speaker box and tells her assistant to bring Hamilton in.

The assistant knocks on the door and opens it for Hamilton to enter.

Georgina turns to Smith, "Before he makes his presentation, I want you to know how helpful he has been in organizing the Total Brain Coaching Workshops."

"Thank you, Georgina," the young man enters the conversation enthusiastically. "It's a pleasure to be a part of SMITH & HATHAWAY and I'm excited to see how the Total Brain Coaching Workshops make use of the latest advances in business, especially the Agile Manifesto, which helps to reinforce the habits needed to create a mindset of greater responsiveness to the customer."

"Perhaps," she gently interrupts him, "you'll explain to Mr. Smith what you mean by the Agile Manifesto."

"Of course! In 2001, seventeen software developers met at a resort in Utah to discuss software development methods, and created *The Manifesto for Agile Software Development*. Agile uses specific procedures, such as Extreme Programming and Kanban, to speed up software development. Agile principles and practices have now greatly expanded and they are applied to many areas of management."

"Really?" Smith is surprised. "What companies are actually using it?"

"Microsoft, Airbnb, Etsy, Lyft, John Deere, Menlo Innovations, Saab, Samsung, Spotify, Tesla, Uber, and many others."

Smith swallows his shock.

"In fact, I predict that any company that uses software development or information technology will," Hamilton declares, throwing his arms up in a dramatic gesture, "eventually have to adopt an Agile mindset! Otherwise, they won't be able to compete in today's dynamic markets which are finally focusing on customers' needs. Would you like to hear all 12 of the principles of the Manifesto?" he asks eagerly.

Smith squirms in his chair.

"Perhaps," suggests Georgina, "you could first explain a little about Scrum and how it improves teamwork."

"Scrum, like in rugby?" asks Smith.

"The same word but a different meaning," Hamilton explains. "Scrum is an innovative, flexible system for improving team collaboration. It's one of the most commonly used tools in Agile software development."

"But we're not a software development company," objects Smith.

"Not yet, anyway." Hamilton laughs. "For some time you've

had a software department that has gone nowhere. Georgina and I have been talking about some new ideas to revive it to give you an advantage in the sports market!"

Georgina interrupts as Smith's eyes begin to roll, "Why don't we save that for another time? Tell us more about Scrum."

"Scrum" he says, "includes a specific set of values, rules, and principles. The five main values are said to be focus, respect, openness, courage, and commitment. The rules recommend that the ideal size of a team should be between three and nine members and it should consist of members who have different skills, creating what's called a 'cross-functional team.' Typically, the team prioritizes product development into smaller iterative time increments called 'Sprints', which can last about two or three weeks. Whatever specific product they come up with is then shown to the stakeholder or customer, for immediate feedback before developing the next part of the project. The principles include openness through transparency, inspection, and adaptation."

He pauses to take a deep breath before continuing. "There are other important features of Scrum. Every day, for example, there's a brief 15-minute "Stand Up" meeting in which all the members of the team actually stand up and share ideas and concerns about how their project is going. This helps to clear up misunderstandings and improve communication. At the end of a two or three week period, the team has a special meeting to discuss how they can improve their own teamwork."

He continues, "Two people act as critical facilitators in any Scrum team. First, there's a Scrum Master, who coaches the whole team and ensures that all the Agile principles are being used. Second, there's a Product Owner, who defines what the specific project is, and ensures that the team is always working towards a practical and customer-relevant goal."

"Scrum sounds like a very well-organized system," comments Smith. "Do you think we could use it at SMITH & HATHAWAY?"

"Good question! It's certainly one of many that could be used. From what I've been learning about Total Brain Coaching, it helps to first change the mindset of a company so that it becomes easier to introduce Agile management tools like Scrum, which has the added value of helping everyone understand the underlying Energy State of each team member."

"I see," says Smith. *I guess I underestimated Hamilton.* "So, by knowing the Energy State of your key employees, you are better able to appreciate who they are and create a more harmonious team. Obviously, picking a team of the smartest and most compatible people would be the best choice." He looks over at Georgina.

"Google conducted an experiment in 2012," she says, "called Project Aristotle. The results were quite interesting. They studied 180 teams and found that the main factor which distinguished high-performance teams from dysfunctional teams wasn't intelligence. It was how the team members treated each other. The five factors which were the most important were: psychological safety, dependability, structure and clarity, meaning, and impact. The team members had to be sensitive to each other in order to be able to communicate effectively, and the work had to be important enough so that they were really engaged in it."

"Interesting," comments Smith. "What do they mean by psychological safety?"

"Simply put, psychological safety is when every team member can say what they really feel with no fear of negative consequences. You need to treat other team members the way they want and need to be treated, not the way that you think they should be treated. It's a breakthrough in workplace relationships. Total Brain Coaching," Georgina tells him, "gives you, as the coach, a huge advantage since you understand the Energy State of each team member, which means that you are in an ideal position to help build psychological safety."

"Can you give me an example?" he asks.

She responds, "Let's say that a team is trying to create a new training program. The V Energy person on the team is bubbling with ideas and needs to be allowed to participate early in the discussion. Once you acknowledge their ideas, the V will then be able to listen to the rest of the group and make creative contributions.

"A P Energy State team member will want to get straight to the point. If the discussion leads in too many directions, the person will try to exert her or his own strong opinions. It's especially important for them to have a specific agenda. You may need to help them keep the discussion focused from the beginning.

"A K Energy State person will need to present their position more slowly, going into great detail. Extra time is important for the K person to present their ideas and also to make decisions."

"This sounds like a lot of babysitting," Smith complains. "I'm used to giving orders and having them followed."

"I understand," Georgina tells him. "But a good leader must help the individuals in a team reach a consensus. In order to do this, trust must exist and trust can only be achieved when each person's attributes and feelings are understood and appreciated."

"How long is it all going to take?" Smith asks.

"Each team is different. Once you understand who the team is really composed of, you can help them work more coherently together. The key is to make sure that everyone stays in good balance. This is why we also coach each team member individually. A V Energy State person who is imbalanced, for example, will often speak too fast and too frequently, and drive everyone crazy, especially a slower K Energy State person. I don't think I have to tell you what happens when a P Energy person goes out of balance!"

"You do not," he agrees. "I'm intimately familiar with the result of being an imbalanced P."

She laughs, "So you understand why keeping everyone in balance is the first job of a Total Brain Coach and that this inevitably involves creating better habits of communication. Everybody needs to have a sense of the whole, as well as a higher purpose. In Total Brain Coaching, the habits of the individuals and teams have to be aligned with the goals of the company."

She adds, "One of the great stories in sports history is how nine working-class boys, part of the University of Washington's rowing team, showed the world at the 1936 Berlin Olympics what true coherence really meant. No one ever expected them to defeat the elite teams of the East Coast and Great Britain, but with a single intensely focused intention they went on to defeat Adolf Hitler's

German rowing team."

She turns to Hamilton, who has been silent for some time. "You've made a good contribution today and I know that there are still more ideas you want to present."

He nods, pleased.

"Why don't we resume this discussion after we have conducted more workshops, Mr. Smith?"

He agrees. And as they stand up, he reflects. *There well may be more to young Hamilton than meets the eye.*

Following Georgina out, a black and white photo on the wall catches his attention. It is an image of Georgina, sitting apparently at ease in a lawn chair, in the presence of the Queen of England and her family.

CHAPTER 8

TOTAL BRAIN DECISION MAKING

Coherent Networks Enhance Performance

Memo: April 27
From: J.P. Smith
To: Georgina

> 1. Need to hear latest report on results of Total Brain Coaching Workshops over last two weeks
>
> 2. Please keep Hamilton presentation short

A t the conference table, Smith and Georgina are having a discussion.

"We're lucky that Greedley has taken so long in making his final offer to Superflex," Smith says.

She agrees. "It's also fortunate that as a result, we've had the opportunity to offer more workshops!"

"From the feedback I've received," he tells her, "the employees seem very happy with them."

She nods. "Now, if you don't mind, I would like Hamilton to come in for a few minutes to give you a brief report."

He shrugs. "Okay, if you think it will help. But please, don't let him go on too long. There are still a lot of fires to put out."

He presses a button on his intercom and Caroline brings Hamilton in. The young man marches across the floor like a Marine reporting to headquarters and immediately starts talking. "I want to present Ray Dalio's latest management ideas to you and explain how they relate to Total Brain Coaching. You know Ray Dalio, don't you, Mr. Smith?"

"No," Smith replies, trying not to be critical, "not personally."

"Dalio founded the largest hedge fund in the world," Hamilton tells him, "and is one of the most influential people. He is probably best known for his best-selling book, Principles, which talks about radical truth and transparency in business. His system has reinforced the habits of trust and openness, which have created a more agile mindset for his company."

An image of the guerrilla leader Che Guevara, complete with black beret and camo fatigues, pops into Smith's mind.

Georgina interrupts his thoughts. "It might be good to define what Dalio means by radical."

"Of course," replies Hamilton, "I'm all for definitions! Dalio explains that being radically truthful and transparent with your colleagues helps the decision making process because it allows everyone to understand what everyone else is thinking."

"In other words," says Smith, "It promotes better communication and, therefore, trust."

"Exactly," Hamilton confirms. "I know you are intimately familiar with the traditional decision making processes of management, Mr. Smith, in which a strategic plan is developed and carefully monitored. You analyze priorities, ensure that you have proper resources, and develop reliable procedures."

"I'm familiar with that," Smith says. "And as far as I can tell, our company has a great strategic plan, but our ability to make good decisions and achieve objectives isn't all that it could be."

"Dalio believes," Hamilton goes on eagerly, "that when it comes to making hard decisions, like eliminating jobs, for instance, there must be open discussions. He quotes Winston Churchill: 'There is no worse course in leadership than to hold out false hopes soon to be swept away!' "

"The tough love approach," laughs Smith.

"Dalio uses those very words!" Hamilton continues excitedly. "He says that radical transparency forces issues, no matter how uncomfortable, to the surface, including mistakes and weaknesses. And this helps to create the kind of understanding that naturally leads to improvements.

"Many people, he explains, believed that his system would never work in practice, but his experience proved them wrong. He also says that radical transparency is not total transparency. It has a particular scope, which may not include people's personal lives. Within certain boundaries, however, it allows people to express what they're feeling.

"Dalio speaks about the value of having a final decision which is based on the merit of many competing ideas, rather than the opinion of one individual. This means that the final decision becomes the result of an open discussion in which all points of view are considered."

Smith turns to Georgina. "What do you think of these radical ideas?"

"I like them," she answers. "They are different from the Agile principles presented before, but they both share the same goal—to create better teamwork and trust. As you well know, Mr. Smith, in business as in personal relationships, trust is vital, and I believe that open discussions help to create trust. The coherence of a company depends upon both trust and confidence in the leader. A crack in the company's coherence can lead to a cascade of problems which will ultimately destroy any chance for success. Once coherence is achieved, making good decisions is as easy as putting," she smiles.

He makes a sarcastic face. "Maybe as easy as you make a putt!"

"There are hidden aspects of decision making," she adds.

"What do you mean?" asks Hamilton.

"Normally, we make decisions in a linear fashion." Georgina tells him. "We gather bits and pieces of information and weigh them together like some kind of mathematical formula. But if we change our habits we create new neural pathways in the brain which allow us to think more comprehensively and improve performance."

"New neural pathways?" repeats Hamilton. "That sounds intriguing to me."

"The human mind," she explains, "has enormous potential. We really are using only a small portion of our brain. When we learn to develop coherent super neural networks in our brain, we become more creative and inclusive in our decision making.

"For certain geniuses, ideas flow naturally," Georgina continues. "Take the example of Mozart. Many of his compositions were said to come to his mind already finished before he committed them to paper. He didn't study or aim at originality. Let me read you a quote."

Taking out her cell phone, she locates a webpage and reads:

> When I am ..... completely myself, entirely alone... or during the night when I cannot sleep, it is on such occasions that my ideas flow best and most abundantly. Whence and how these ideas come I know not nor can I force them.

"And," she says, again looking at her phone, "let me quote Albert Einstein:

> The supreme task of the physicist is to arrive at those universal elementary laws from which the cosmos can be built up by pure deduction. There is no logical path to these laws; only intuition, resting on sympathetic understanding of experience, can reach them.

"The creative process has always been valued by great minds. When our brain behaves coherently, it is able to perform at a high level without our even thinking about it."

"Can you give me an example in sports?" asks Smith.

"Are you familiar with the famous soccer player Pelé?"

Smith and Hamilton both nod yes.

"Do you know why he was so good?" she asks.

Smith offers, "Maybe because he started young or trained hard?"

"Yes," she says slowly, "but Pelé was something more. What

people noticed about his amazing performances were his creativity, improvisation, and ability to make instant decisions. He would feign one way and then, with extraordinary agility, move in another direction. He was able to anticipate his opponents' movement and he became one of the most prolific scorers ever. In the 1958 World Cup against Sweden, when he was only 17 years old, he flicked the ball over a defender and scored. For his second goal, he looped the ball over the keeper's head. Sigge Parling, his Swedish opponent, said after that game that he wanted to applaud Pelé.

"He was on the winning team of three World Cup events. The last in 1970 was when Brazil played Italy in Mexico City. Pelé was past his prime but he scored the opening goal with a header, and then made two crucial assists. In the final goal he was in virtually perfect synchronization with his teammate Carlos Albert. Some people consider that this was the best team goal ever made because it involved so many players. At the last moment Pelé made a blind pass that went right to where Carlos Alberto was running, and Carlos made a perfect shot to the corner of the goal. You can see the whole thing on YouTube. Today there are other amazing players, for example Lionel Messi."

"That all sounds great," Hamilton asks, "but is there any science behind it?"

"Brain scientists have conducted extensive studies on intuition and they suggest that intuitive decision making is controlled by specific networks in the brain that are activated from a perception of coherence in the environment."

"Please," Smith exclaims, "no more brain science!"

"There are many ways, Mr. Smith, to make a decision," Georgina tells him. "The very best way is to be able to make use of a highly coherent brain. Too many decisions are made when people are tired and using only a tiny amount of their brain's potential. There are certain situations in which stress may be helpful. It can focus your attention on an immediate solution, especially when bodily harm may be involved. However, when we over-respond to normal situations in a stressful manner, this dramatically modifies our brain functioning and disables the neural networks that allow us to make accurate and comprehensive decisions. Stress can also disrupt other parts of our body, like our digestion. The gut and brain are intimately connected. If we change our habits and balance our Energy State we counteract the effects of stress and improve all aspects of health."

Caroline quietly enters the room and hands a phone to Smith. He holds the receiver to his ear for a few moments, then hangs up and turns to Georgina.

"So much for radical transparency," he says. "I think we have a spy in our midst."

Georgina and Hamilton look at him, startled.

"Ray Dalio," Hamilton interjects, "is very clear that transparency only works when people respect the moral integrity of the company. If somebody is leaking information, it's unethical behavior and they should be dismissed."

"You're right," Smith says firmly.

"Let's close our meeting now. I need to find out what's going on."

"Of course," Georgina agrees. "And please block out some time for us to meet tomorrow, Mr. Smith."

Hamilton hurries out of the room and Georgina stays behind.

"I know we are in the middle of an emergency," Smith tells her, "but I want you to know that I managed to hold myself back from controlling everything during several meetings today, and I took the time to listen to what the others were talking about."

He pauses. "It felt good."

"I'm impressed, Mr. Smith, and I'm looking forward to hearing more about your progress once this security issue is resolved. We have a lot to discuss."

At a time like this, he thinks, *what more is there to discuss? I need action. A quick trip to Fort Knox would do it!*

CHAPTER 9

IN THE ZONE

Going Beyond

Memo April 28
From: J.P. Smith
To: Georgina

    1. Greedley's concerns with Arnold being a spy remain unproven

    2. Any ideas for proposal to Superflex

S mith's intercom buzzes demandingly. "Yes?" he says curtly into the speaker.

    "Dame Georgina and Hamilton Jr. are here to see you."

"Thanks, Caroline," he responds in a friendlier voice.

Georgina enters the room with Hamilton close behind. Sitting down beside Smith, her posture is attentive. Her eyes are on Hamilton as he begins his presentation.

The young man walks around the office for the next forty minutes, lecturing them on how the largest and fastest growing firms on the planet are using Agile management practices. He cites several articles that explain how the old bureaucratic models of 20th century business are being replaced by this new style of management, which can adapt quickly to changing markets using networks of small teams who are customer oriented, even "customer obsessed." Again he cites the five largest companies on the planet as examples.

"How did these companies get their managers and employees to adopt such radically new principles and practices?" Smith asks.

"The path to success has been unique for each company," Hamilton replies. "They were faced with different situations, different challenges, but their aims were similar—to unfold the full potential of each employee, cultivate meaningful work relationships, and create a culture focused on giving value to the customer in the quickest and most responsive manner.

"And not all of these firms credit their changes to Agile. Amazon, for example, has its own terminology, such as 'two-pizza teams,' and people talk about the 'Google Way.' But most of them have a comparable internal structure, consisting of a coherent network of autonomous teams devoted to the customer."

"Do other companies also use Agile practices?"

"I recently read a number of articles in Forbes," Hamilton answers, "by a Steve Denning, who says that Airbnb, Etsy, Lyft, Menlo Innovations, Saab, Samsung, Spotify, Tesla, Uber, and Warby Parker all use Agile. He mentions a survey which found that 90% of senior executives today want their company to become Agile, but fewer than 10% have attained this goal.

"Denning explains that the term 'Agile' is often used without an agreement as to its meaning, and that it's important to look beyond what the firms are saying and see what they are actually doing. He gives the example of Walmart before 2016, when they incorporated some of the procedures of Agile without having an Agile mindset. The teams were using Agile processes but the managers were still in a bureaucratic top-down management style. This was changed the following year and the result was a marked improvement in sales, although most would agree they are far from an Agile transformation. If you look at Sam Walton's original ideal you do find that they include some Agile principles.

"At a recent international Agile conference," he continues, "a number of presentations were about 'Fake Agile.' There are many types of Fake Agile: for example, a firm might adopt Agile for their software division but not for the other branches of the company. There are other similar terms like 'Badly Done Agile,' 'Dark Agile,' and 'Cosmetic Agile,' each referring to a different situation in which what is purported be 'Agile' is actually not true Agile. Dark Agile, for instance, is when a manager uses meetings that were designed to help improve the performance of teams, to, instead, identify poorly performing members."

"That's disgusting," Smith responds.

"Apparently," continues Hamilton, "the U.S. Department of Defense has now issued specific guidelines for detecting Fake Agile."

"Are you advising me not to adopt Agile?" Smith asks in disbelief.

"What do you think, Mr. Smith?"

"I think that Agile is a good fit for our company," he says. "And if we use it along with Total Brain Coaching we can accelerate changing and improving the habits and mindset of our employees and teams."

"That's a very perceptive answer. There is a dynamic interaction between mindset and habits. In a growth-oriented mindset everyone is more open to adopting new habits. Remember your habits shape how you think, how you communicate, how you perform, and how well you interact with others. When you adopt new habits, which help to balance your Energy State, you naturally have access to greater energy and creativity. This helps you to move to an even more flexible mindset which is responsive to change. There's a positive feedback loop in which habit change helps to improve mindset, and a more growth-oriented mindset helps to change habits.

"Total Brain Coaching," she continues, "uses the power of attention to create coherence. As we talked about in Kauai, Mr. Smith, it begins with a simple ancient principle, 'What you put your attention on grows stronger.' "

Hamilton jumps in. "You're talking about the Hawthorne Effect, right? In the 1930s Elton Mayo did a number of experiments at the Hawthorne Works of Western Electric's plant near Cicero, Illinois.

"In one study they turned up the lights in the plant to see if productivity would increase. And it did. Why? Not because the workers liked brighter light, but because the researchers were putting their attention on the workers. When they turned the lights back down, productivity went up again. The conclusion was that the most important factor in increasing productivity was personal attention!"

"Very good!" Georgina praises him. The young man laps it up like a puppy drinking gravy.

She continues, "In Total Brain Coaching, we manage the flow of attention to help create good habits."

"This sounds a lot like behavioral management theory," Hamilton comments. "HR people are always trying to do things to improve creativity or help everyone become more sensitive to each other."

"This is something quite different, however," Georgina tells him. "I'm not talking about making a mood of being more sensitive or more energetic, 'faking it'. And there's no 'trying' involved. Think of Yoda: 'Do or not do. There is no try!' "

Smith can't help but grin and Hamilton laughs out loud.

"What I'm talking about," Georgina explains, "is waking up inside and nourishing your self-awareness. Total Brain Coaching helps people maintain a balanced Energy State. When your Energy State becomes more coherent, you are happier, more awake, able to communicate in a more ideal way, and make positive changes in your life. By understanding yourself and being in good balance, you can give more energy and help to your team. All these changes take time but the ultimate result is a dynamic, coherent team.

"Are you ready for yet another sports analogy?"

"Sure."

"Great athletes in championship teams have described the experience of 'clicking' together. There are moments when each player spontaneously and automatically senses the next move of his or her teammates. Before such players make a pass, for instance, they know exactly where their teammate is going to be. In a state of complete harmony and coordination, they are able to make outstanding individual shots and participate in remarkable teamwork.

"Wayne Gretzky," she goes on, "is one the most famous ice hockey players, who is known for his amazing passes. And do you know what he did before a game? When everyone else was horsing around, he would sit quietly, relaxed in mind and body, and 'play' the coming game in his mind, mentally rehearsing perfect plays. When he was out on the rink, the coherence and preparedness of his mind and body allowed magic to happen!"

Smith has to ask: "You know Gretzky?"

"Oh," she says, with a nonchalant movement of her hand, "I knew him when he was young."

"I really like your sports examples," says Hamilton.

"Good! And a video makes my point even clearer." She opens her computer and the two men move closer to the screen to watch Willie Mays make an unbelievable catch. Georgina stops the recording and rewinds it slightly.

"Watch it again," she suggests, "and tell me what you notice."

The video plays again. Smith says, "I'm not sure, except that it sure was a great catch!"

"How does this relate to performance in a business?" Hamilton asks her.

"Just watch." This time she stops the video at a split screen picture. On one half of the screen is a batter and on the other, Willie in centerfield. When the video moves in slow motion, Smith can clearly see Willie begin racing to his left as the ball is hit.

"Let's run it once more at regular speed," she suggests, "this time with the volume on, so that you can hear the impact of the bat hitting the ball."

Smith watches and listens carefully.

"At the crack of the bat," she points out, "Willie begins running to his left. Almost before the ball leaves the bat, he has computed the distance and direction and runs on a deliberate path. He effortlessly catches the ball in full stride."

"Amazing!" Smith nearly shouts.

Georgina elaborates, "As soon as the ball was hit, Willie had enough sensory input to know exactly where to run and how fast. Such athletes have a very high degree of mind-body coordination."

"To play at the highest levels of performance," she tells them, "requires that the mind and body are coherent. Such coherence can only come from silence, from a relaxed alert brain. What do you think Willie Mays was thinking about before the ball was hit?"

The men are silent and Georgina answers her own question. "Not much!" She laughs.

"If he was trying to think at that moment it would have interfered with his brain's ability to compute," she explains. "Thinking would be like an extraneous noise that would break his connection to deeper levels of awareness. The fielder has to be alert, but he must also be in a relaxed and easy state, physically and mentally, with no distractions or any straining about what to do next. He is maximally prepared, in a state of restful alertness. It's the same in any sport."

She pauses thoughtfully and says, "The main obstacles to achieving coherence are stress and fatigue."

Smith nods in agreement. "Often when I'm trying to go to sleep after a stressful day my head is buzzing like a beehive."

"When you've have a tough day," she explains, "there may still be some incoherence in your nervous system at night. Your body will naturally try to throw off the stresses you incurred during the day and this activity of the nervous system can cause your mind to be agitated. In other words, there really is an intimate relationship between your mind and body. What you want is to create an ideal state of mind-body coordination, characterized by coherence and restful alertness, rather than incoherence and stress."

"So, what can we do," asks Hamilton, "flip a switch in our brain?"

"That's a good image," she says. "In a way that is precisely what you do. There are many different ways of influencing the integration of the mind and body. Athletes achieve greater mind-body coordination through long hours of training, which creates muscle memory and positive habits. Then, when they are in a competitive situation they don't have to think about what moves to make. Their body automatically knows what to do."

"Are you suggesting," asks Hamilton, "that the company adopt an exercise training program?"

"No, the technique I have in mind is much more profound. Exercise is a valuable part of improving our health and I am happy to recommend a very effective program. What I want you and your employees to do is a simple mental technique which improves all areas of individual life, and which simultaneously generates maximum coherence for the company."

"Is this the technique that you were talking about when we were in Kauai?" Smith asks. "Meditation, right?"

"Yes. Transcendental Meditation."

"Oh," Hamilton brightens, "I read about that in Ray Dalio's book. He attributes much of his success to practicing Transcendental Meditation and he's also part of a nonprofit called the David Lynch Foundation, which uses the Transcendental Meditation program to help at-risk children.

"A lot of companies these days encourage their employees to do some form of meditation. There are even designated meditation rooms. I looked into Transcendental Meditation and I read a bunch of scientific articles. TM has been shown to improve creativity, memory, and learning ability, and it lowers cholesterol levels and blood pressure. It's even supposed to increase longevity!"

"Hey," Smith exclaims, "if you could give me a pill that would do all that I'd gladly take it. Does TM really do all that?"

"What if I could prove to you," Georgina says, "that during TM your body produces physiological changes that act like a wonder pill, improving your memory and learning ability and lowering blood pressure—with no side effects?"

"Are you saying that I wouldn't have to go on a special diet or sleep on a bed of nails?" he probes.

"No special diet," she smiles, "no sleeping on a bed of nails. Total Brain Coaching utilizes a variety of optional tools and one of the most important is the Transcendental Meditation program.

TM allows the mind to naturally settle down, while at the same time remaining alert, and ultimately creating a highly coherent brain state."

"But if our mind has to be completely silent in order to be perfectly coherent, how can we get anything done?" Hamilton asks. "Wouldn't we all just be sitting around, feeling rested but not accomplishing anything?"

She laughs. "That hasn't happened yet. The mind and nervous system become experienced at functioning coherently, even in activity, which is the basis for great achievement in sports and in life. In order to generate a powerful level of group coherence, the TM technique should be taught to as many people as possible in a company."

"Interesting," murmurs Hamilton.

"The real key to management is to do everything possible to strengthen the collective coherence of the group. In the last few weeks you have begun to create teams in your company, which are beginning to work more effectively together. I've seen a kind of threshold effect in companies that have embraced Total Brain Coaching. When a certain percentage of people begin to change, the whole company takes off."

There is a knock at the door.

"Yes?"

"There's a call for Dame Georgina," says Caroline.

"Don't tell me," he jokes, "it's the Emperor of Japan!"

"No, sir," she replies in hushed tones. "It's the Dalai Lama calling from the Dharamsala."

CHAPTER 10

SAMURAI NEGOTIATION

Agility and Coherence

Memo: July 27
From: Anne Bright, Chief Legal Counsel
To: J.P. Smith

1. Superflex is not happy with Greedley after more than 3 months, he keeps changing the agreement

2. We are exploring new approaches to the deal

The past three months have gone by quickly, Smith reflects as he waits for the meeting to begin. It had been an inspirational period and reminds him of one of those old fashioned barn-raisings, with everyone getting together and pitching in. *It feels,* he thinks, *like real progress.*

Total Brain Coaching Workshops were given to a number of employees, resulting in improvement in both individual and team performance. Smith had even started to change his own leadership style. He faithfully checked in with Georgina every day for the first week, and now he's doing it once a week. He no longer sits in meetings interrupting everyone and trying to control everything. He is actually able to be quiet and really listen to the discussion.

He contributes only at the end of a meeting by summarizing the results and delegating responsibility.

As part of the Total Brain Coaching program, Georgina had instructed and encouraged him to coach others. He was apprehensive when she assigned Doug Hatchett to him as his first 'coachee'. But Doug was actually interested in changing his anger issues and their coaching sessions were remarkably smooth. Smith had begun by asking him to write, in the center of a page, what he would most like to change. Doug wrote—reduce anger meltdowns. Smith then asked him to write down the different approaches he had tried before, which included anger management classes. He then asked Doug if there was any other approach he would like to try, and Doug told him that he was open to new ideas. They discussed what caused a P Energy State person to become imbalanced. Doug listed the big three—not eating on time, spicy food, and overheating. He then decided on his new habit—making sure that he ate lunch on time.

Smith checked in with Doug every day after work to see how he was doing. He didn't have a perfect record but after a few weeks Doug was able to adopt the new habit and it was already helping to reduce his meltdowns. Their coaching sessions brought them closer together and Doug was now a more effective member of the executive team.

Smith's thoughts are interrupted as Hamilton Jr. bursts into the room, with Georgina following quietly behind.

"I had no idea that you had such brilliant software teams, Mr. Smith!" the young man exclaims.

"Thanks," says Smith. "Frankly, I don't even know anyone in that department."

"Ben Arnold recruited them about a year ago," Hamilton tells him enthusiastically, "but they weren't making much progress. The Total Brain Coaching Workshops have changed everything. They're on track now and producing an amazing app!"

As glad as Smith is to hear a success story, the overall fate of his company still weighs heavily on his mind.

"This could be a game changer, J.P.," Georgina comments.

Smith smiles widely, thinking to himself, *I fail to see how some software app is going to turn things around, but I know she wants me to put attention on our wins, so I'm going to be positive!*

"Perhaps Hamilton can tell us more about it?" he suggests.

The young man doesn't need a second invitation. "First of all, the software teams made no progress for months. Ben Arnold had them working on some elaborate scheme to improve customer service.

"You should have seen the software office. Before, there was a huge chart on the wall, using a top-down Waterfall method, which tediously details the project. It's like a picture of some prehistoric dinosaur. And for some bizarre reason no team ever actually received feedback from the customer service people! To make matters worse, Hatchett was taking away the top programmers for his own pet projects, completely disrupting the teams."

Smith gropes for a positive outcome. "So, what's changed?"

"You! You changed, Mr. Smith!" Hamilton exclaims. "You offered them Total Brain Coaching Workshops which helped them create new positive habits. The whole atmosphere changed. They had more energy and creativity and were excited to look into some of the Agile practices that help improve teamwork."

"This might be a good time to refresh Mr. Smith's memory regarding Agile," Georgina suggests encouragingly.

Hamilton explains, "Agile is a set of principles on how to effectively create software. Agile teamwork programs like Scrum give the programmers immediate feedback from the customers. And Agile is being used for more than software development. In fact, it may well be one of the main reasons that Microsoft is so successful. In 2011, they announced their commitment to Agile and by 2015, one of their divisions of hundreds of teams was involved in an Agile transformation.

"In Agile, each team has a certain degree of autonomy and self-organizing power in terms of how they get the work done, which helps to motivate them. Each team has to know what the other teams are doing and there are meetings specifically designed to ensure that everyone is coordinated and accountable. There is continuous feedback from the customer. One of the reasons Microsoft was so successful was that they were using teams even before they adopted Agile. It still took time and effort on the part of the leadership, who made numerous changes, including a whole new workspace designed to encourage Agile principles."

The good Dame adds, "The current CEO of Microsoft, Satya Nadella, is an advocate of Agile principles. Shortly after he became CEO, he explained how he was going to enliven the corporate culture with a mission, 'to empower every person and organization on the planet to achieve more.' Instead of becoming a bureaucratic Brontosaurus, Microsoft is now a highly coherent group of dynamic teams ready to move like empathetic raptors in a split second!"

Images of Jurassic Park flood Smith's mind and he exclaims. "That sounds great to me!"

"Since Satya Nadella became CEO," Georgina tells him, "Microsoft's value has increased by about a quarter of a trillion dollars. One of the first things he did was to have his top executives read Marshall Rosenberg's book, *Nonviolent Communication*. Nadella changed the corporate culture by changing the mindset of his employees."

Hamilton interjects. "For Agile to work you have to change the culture of the whole company. It's ideal when a leader, embraces a new idea and leads by example and experience.

"By offering Total Brain Coaching Workshops, Mr. Smith," Hamilton continued, "you've done exactly that. Your employees are discovering who they are, how to maximize their energy, and how to communicate better. You are creating a more open and transparent environment.

"And this is only the beginning of the transformation. Changing habits takes place on three levels—individual, team, and organization. Georgina has coached you and you are coaching others. And because, as the leader of the company, you have included your executive team as well as other teams, you have already started to change the habits of the entire corporate culture from the top down and from the bottom up."

Hamilton is excited. "Your software division teams have been empowered to produce manageable pieces of software of real value. The teams are communicating well among themselves, and each is accountable for their results. There is already an amazing degree of resonance. The app they're developing could really increase the market share of our company!"

"I want you to know, Hamilton," says Smith, "I'm delighted with your work here. I'm still a student of Total Brain Coaching myself and I don't have all the answers, but I hope this app does everything you say it will."

"That's an excellent attitude, Mr. Smith," Hamilton remarks. "I believe a real leader is able to ask questions and is constantly working on his or her mindset."

The intercom sounds and they hear the quiet voice of Smith's assistant, Caroline. "I'm sorry to interrupt your meeting Mr. Smith but—"

"—I know," he remarks jokingly, "it's the White House again for Dame Georgina!"

"No," she continues, "its Anne Bright. She wants to join your meeting. She has some important information on the Superflex deal."

"Send her right in!"

He turns to Georgina, "I hope you don't mind."

"By all means, have her join us."

Ms. Bright comes into the room. "I apologize for interrupting but I thought that you would want to know the latest developments in negotiations with Superflex since it involves Hamilton and Georgina."

Smith regards her intently. "Tell us everything."

"You are well aware that we can't match Greedley's offer to Superflex. And, as you know, their new board member is your own sister-in-law." Anne pauses.

"She's the one who is responsible for delaying their negotiation, and these delays have given us time to learn more about Superflex."

Smith shudders at the mention of his sister-in-law. Seraphim is a formidable opponent. I bet Musashi would have thought twice before facing her!

"Do you remember what I said about Musashi, Mr. Smith?" asks Georgina interrupting his thoughts.

Again, he thinks, she's reading my mind!

"One of Musashi's most important practices as a swordsman," she reminds him, "was to learn everything he could about his opponent before their confrontation."

He takes this as a cue to ask, "What did you learn about Superflex?"

"That the money isn't as important as we thought," Anne answers. "They've been looking for a long-term partner so I invited some of their executives to attend a few Total Brain Coaching Workshops. They were impressed. Do you know what they like the most?"

"What?" he asks expectantly.

"The new app we're creating. They think it could revolutionize the sports and health world!"

Smith turns to Hamilton. "What makes this app so special?"

"After the Total Brain Coaching Workshops," the young man tells him, "the teams decided to redesign the app so that it could assess the customer's Energy State and offer individualized sports and health recommendations based on this analysis. They also added an AI feature that coaches the customer on how to change his particular habits."

Smith lights up. "Artificial intelligence, that's interesting!"

"Yes, it is," replies Hamilton. "We gave the app to a focus group and after a week interviewed them."

He chuckles, "My favorite comment was that the app gives the customer Jedi mind power. But the most common comments were that it enabled them to increase their energy level and helped them identify the exercise and sport programs that suited them personally. It also helped them understand what steps were necessary to adopt a new habit. They also discovered how to communicate better—with their friends, fellow team members, their boss, their spouse, and their kids. A few said that the app even helped improve their digestion."

"I'm not surprised," Georgina says. "We know that Total Brain Coaching includes detailed knowledge about the gut-brain axis and incorporates time-tested recommendations to improve digestion and diet."

Smith is impressed and a little surprised.

"This puts us in a unique position to bargain with Superflex," Anne tells them. "Rather than a lot of money up front, they want a piece of our app. They would also like access to our business expertise and experience running Total Brain Coaching Workshops."

Smith and Georgina exchange a knowing glance.

"The more we can learn about them," Anne says, "the better position we are in to negotiate a win-win agreement. Seraphim's presence in Greedley's company has caused so much confusion, it's helping us immensely."

So, thinks Smith, *my arch nemesis is actually helping us.* A wild snort of laughter escapes him.

CHAPTER 11

THE COHERENCE EFFECT

Coherence Creates Success

Memo: Aug 25
From: J.P. Smith
To: Board of Directors

    1. Discuss purchase of Superflex

    2. Finalize termination of President Ben Arnold

Two members of Smith's board of directors are doodling on their notepads, while the others stare stonily ahead. Hamilton Ridgeway Sr., a narrow gray-haired man with a crisp military mustache, looks periodically out the window. No one engages Smith as he enters. *Obviously they are worried about the purchase of Superflex!*

Ben Arnold bursts into the room. His dramatic entrance has every appearance of a last-minute attempt to keep his job.

"What do you want, Ben?" Smith asks warily. "Can't you see this is a private board meeting?"

"I have information that's vital to the board's impending decision."

He addresses the board, "Please hear me out. I believe there will be no need to vote."

"No need to vote?" Smith repeats, eyeing him coolly. "Let's have it, Ben."

Arnold's story unfolds. "Eight months ago, I made a terrible mistake and misused my position at SMITH & HATHAWAY to obtain valuable information for my own personal gain." He takes a deep breath. "I never intended to be an inside trader, but we had a family emergency and I had huge medical bills, with no way to pay them."

He holds up a hand. "I know that's no excuse. I thought that it wouldn't hurt to bend the rules just once, and I believed that I could cover my tracks."

He rubs his eyes. "My conscience ate at me. I hated my dishonesty and I felt like my whole life was falling apart. Then something happened that gave me the guts to face up to what I'd done."

Smith clears his throat, breaking the thick silence in the room.

"That something," Ben continues, "was Mr. Smith's effort to revive SMITH & HATHAWAY. If he could make positive changes in the face of huge odds, I figured that I could face the SEC. It wasn't an easy decision, but it was right. The problem was that I had a friend who was also involved in the trade and I couldn't go through with my disclosure plans without implicating him. In fact, his involvement is far greater than mine and it turned out that the SEC was already closing in on him. A couple of weeks ago this person agreed to cooperate with me. I wanted to tell everyone right away, especially you, Mr. Smith, but I was sworn to secrecy until the SEC reached their final decision."

Again no one says a word. After a few moments, Smith says, "I wish you had come to me earlier when we could have avoided losing you. But I appreciate your being honest with us now."

"Thank you," Arnold pauses. "A few minutes ago I received a call from one of the SEC investigators. It turns out that their decision on my wrongdoing may be more positive than I expected. The reason I came to you today is to report their judgment on Greedley."

There's a feeling of excitement in the room as he continues, "It was Paul Greedley who helped me gather the inside information."

They all speak at once and Smith raises his hands for quiet.

"The point I'm trying to make," Ben goes on, "is that all of Greedley's transactions are being scrutinized by the SEC. They won't let him, or any group he is connected with, participate in the purchase of Superflex. I have been told they are bringing charges against him and he will immediately be asked to resign."

An atmosphere of relief and lightness fills the room. "Thank you, Ben," says Smith. "We appreciate your being so open. And the SEC's decision about Greedley is welcome news."

There is a spurt of hearty applause from the board.

Smith stands up. "I now officially adjourn this meeting so we can finalize the Superflex deal. Once that's done we are going to celebrate."

Talking excitedly among themselves, the board members leave the room.

Hamilton Ridgeway Sr. comes over to Smith. "I'm very

impressed by the changes in the company" he tells him, "and even more so by the changes I see in my son. Since Hamilton Jr. has been working for you and taking the Total Brain Coaching Workshop, his behavior and mannerisms have changed. He takes time to understand people now, and he wants to bring the best out in each of them. He's actually patient and polite with me! It's remarkable—we haven't been this close in years."

"Your son has a bright future in this company," Smith replies. "I'm thinking about creating a new position for him, VP of Learning and Development."

The older man beams. "I appreciate your confidence in him and I look forward to watching his future in the company. I would actually like to start investing more capital so that you can finalize the purchase of Superflex without hurting current operations, especially the software department which, my son tells me, has come up with a remarkable new app!"

Smiling, Smith replies, "Your investment would be very helpful. I must say that the new app is largely due to the efforts of your son and Dame Georgina St. George."

"Yes, Junior is quite impressed with your consultant."

Smith nods, "We owe her a deep debt of gratitude."

Hamilton Sr. looks around. "Where is she anyway?"

"She's a very private individual," Smith explains, "and asked not to attend the board meeting. "If you will excuse me, Mr. Hamilton, I'll go now and tell her our news. She's waiting in another office."

"By all means. Please thank her on behalf of the board. One of these days I would like to thank her personally for mentoring my son."

"I'll be glad to set that meeting up for you," Smith tells him with a smile.

They shake hands and leave the conference room.

Entering a slightly smaller office Smith announces, "You won't believe what happened, Georgina."

"You have my greatest congratulations!" she responds. "A friend called me with the good news while you were in your meeting."

Ah nuts! I might have known that nothing could escape her network! "And did you also hear about Hamilton Sr.'s offer to invest more money?" he asks.

"No," she says mildly, calm as a Buddha.

A-hah! he thinks. *Maybe she has finally stopped reading my mind.*

He looks at her. "You're not even surprised, are you?

"Oh, Mr. Smith, there are so many factors at work. You've done a magnificent job of creating effective teamwork and reviving the company's performance. You have also changed your own habits and mindset as well as that of your company."

"Tell me," he says, "did you know all along that Ben Arnold was an inside trader and that he would turn himself in?"

"I had absolutely no idea," was the reply.

"Then you admit that it's a surprise?"

"I was always confident of a completely positive conclusion. Whenever a coherent, harmonious group has a clear intention, the results are always remarkable. And I knew that when you added the final coherence tools, great positive changes would follow. It was extremely brave and wise of you, Mr. Smith, to make those changes."

"You are my coach, Georgina, and I believe in you. Please, call me J.P."

She smiles. "You've done very well, J.P, to have created coherence and agility in your company at such a difficult time."

"But," Smith pauses, "now what?"

"Now," she says, "in order for SMITH & HATHAWAY to generate further success, your Total Brain Coaching programs have to stay as relevant and dynamic as they are today."

"I understand. There are a few employees who still haven't taken the Total Brain Coaching Workshops, so we need to remedy that. I guess too, that I have administrative duties to take care of before I can get out on the golf course again!"

"Which reminds me," she says, "would you be interested in a game at a southern course this weekend? It will be just a few friends."

"That's very kind of you, but I may need to meet with Hamilton Sr. Can I get back to you tomorrow?"

She waves a hand. "Of course. Or my assistant will call to see when you're free. My own schedule is a little tight since I'm leaving for Africa soon. The country I was supposed to visit has finished its elections and I have meetings to conclude before I go there next week. You have everything so well in hand at SMITH & HATHAWAY," she concludes, "you don't need me any more!"

"Oh, I don't know about that," he says, "but I'm considerably more confident than when we first met. And I know that I owe you a great deal. Thank you."

They shake hands. "Everything that's been accomplished," she says, "is just the natural result of the Coherence Code."

As he watches her go out the office door, the intercom sounds. "Yes?"

"While you were meeting with Georgina," Caroline tells him, "there was a message for her. I didn't want to interrupt and then she went by so quickly I didn't have a chance to tell her."

"What's the message?"

"It confirmed the time for a golf game this weekend in Augusta, Georgia."

"Augusta?" Smith's interest is sparked. "Who is the message from?"

"It's from a—I believe it's a Mr. Nicklose? I think it's that famous golfer who won so many championships."

"Jack Nicklaus," yells Smith. "Yes!" He jumps up from his chair. *Now that's what I call being in tune with nature!*

ABOUT THE AUTHORS

Dr. Robert Keith Wallace did pioneering research on the Transcendental Meditation technique. His seminal papers—published in *Science, American Journal of Physiology,* and *Scientific American*—on a fourth major state of consciousness supported a new paradigm of mind-body medicine and total brain development. Dr. Wallace is the founding President of Maharishi University of Management and has traveled around the world giving lectures at major universities and institutes on Consciousness-Based health programs. He is currently a Trustee of Maharishi University of Management, and Chairman of the Department of Physiology and Health.

Dr. Wallace has written and co-authored a number of books, the latest of which is *The Rest And Repair Diet: Heal Your Gut, Improve Your Physical and Mental Health, and Lose Weight.*

A former model, Samantha Wallace was featured on the covers of *Vogue, Cosmopolitan,* and *Look* magazine. She is a long time practitioner of Transcendental Meditation, and has a deep understanding of Ayurveda and its relationship to health and well being. Samantha co-authored *Gut Crisis* and *The Rest And Repair*

Diet, which integrate ancient Ayurvedic wisdom with the latest findings in modern medicine.

She is also the co-author of *Quantum Golf,* and was an editor of *Dharma Parenting.* Her most recent book is *Beauty And Being Yourself: A User-Friendly Introduction to Ayurveda And Essential Oil Skincare,* co-authored by Dr. Wallace and Veronica Wells Butler, M.D.

Happily married for over forty years, the Wallaces have a combined family of four children and six grandchildren.

Ted Wallace is currently an Agile Coach at Cambridge Investment Research, Inc. He has completed two Master of Science degrees, one in Computer Science and another in Physiology from Maharishi International University. He is a certified Scrum Master Professional (CSM, CSPO, CSP) and a registered corporate coach (RCC) with thousands of hours of coaching sessions completed. Ted is a former CEO of Maharishi Ayurveda Products International.

Ted and his talented wife, Danielle, have three amazing children, Jace, Kyran, and Myka.

ACKNOWLEDGMENTS

First of all, we thank Jay Marcus for significant contributions to earlier versions of this book, and Rashi Glazer, PhD, for his many insightful suggestions. Special credit goes to Kjell Enhager for his personal golf stories and business knowledge. We thank Huy Nguyen for his inspiring editorial comments. We want to express deep appreciation to Nat Goldhaber for some great conversations about key ideas and for his valuable suggestions. Our thanks to John Wurdeman and Warren Blank for their instructive advice and to Fran Clark and Rick Nakata for proofreading. We also want to recognize our talented friend George Foster for his creative cover. Finally, heartfelt thanks to our friends Kiki and Marc Ellenby for providing us with a writing sanctuary in their comfortable and comforting Miami home.

CHAPTER NOTES

Chapter 1. THE COHERENCE CODE

Employee Net Promoter Score

The Net Promoter Score (NPS) is a way of evaluating employee satisfaction and loyalty on a scale from -100 to +100. The NPS is also used to measure customer satisfaction and loyalty. A Net Promoter Score can be measured by taking a simple survey that asks the question: "Would you recommend this product to your friends or family?" Scores vary depending on how much happiness or satisfaction the company's products bring the customer. Very successful companies have an NPS of 70 or more. A score of minus 30 suggests serious problems in the company.

Bill Russell Quote

This quote was taken from an article in the August 04, 1969 issue of *Sports Illustrated* at https://www.si.com/vault/2016/07/13/im-not-involved-anymore

Chapter 2. GAME OF SWORDS

The Kyoto Resort is a purely fictional hotel located on Kauai, Hawaii.

Chapter 3. ENERGY STATES

Energy States And Ayurveda

Ayurveda is a comprehensive, prevention-oriented system of natural medicine that addresses our body, mind, and environment. In this holistic approach to health, each person is evaluated according to his or her individual mind/body type or nature. Traditionally, the three basic Energy States have been called Vata, Pitta, and Kapha doshas. As much as possible, we abbreviate these words to V for Vata, P for Pitta, and K for Kapha: V, P, and K. In our books *Gut Crisis* and *The Rest And Repair Diet* we use the term Gut/Brain Nature in order to emphasize the importance of the gut-brain axis to your health.

Your Energy State can be determined either by answering a simple questionnaire, or by an examination by a trained Ayurveda expert. Scientific research demonstrates that the Energy State is correlated with individual genetic and physiological measures, and with the composition of the gut bacteria (see the book Total Brain Coaching for more details).

V Energy State

V Energy State individuals are bright, good at creating new ideas and projects, and able to learn quickly. If, however, they become imbalanced, they easily lose their energy and can become fatigued and oversensitive. They may also experience mood swings, and they will then have difficulty in following a project through to the end. The secret for a V person to maintain balance is to follow a good routine. Certain simple dietary and lifestyle changes will also greatly help to rebalance and sustain the energy of a V individual.

<u>V Digestion</u>

V people have a variable appetite and digestive power, strong at one moment and weak at another. If you are a V, you are likely to be a "snacker," who benefits from eating several small nutritious meals throughout the day. Please note that it is important for a V to eat in a quiet environment, away from stress or distractions. When the V Gut is balanced, digestion is good. When it is out of balance, the V individual may experience such symptoms as constipation, indigestion, and gas.

<u>V Exercise</u>

V individuals are attracted to exercise that involves moving quickly but they are not suited for endurance sports. They are sprinters rather than marathoners, and should be careful not to get overtired. Activities such as dancing, paddle boarding, Yoga, and anything that keeps them moving will be good for them. V

Energy State people do well with a moderate, steady, grounding, and warming workout.

V Sleep

A V person has a hard time going to sleep and is susceptible to insomnia. Take extra care to avoid stimulation before bedtime and do something to relax, like taking a warm bath, listening to peaceful music, and using calming aromatherapy.

P Energy State

P Energy State individuals have a great deal of energy and staying power. They can also be very aggressive, and often possess a strong and penetrating intellect. They tend to be well-organized and can be good decision-makers. It is no coincidence that businesspeople and athletes are frequently P individuals. When a P is imbalanced, they may have trouble controlling their anger, or, at the very least, irritation, from time to time. They can also be impatient, difficult to interact with, and controlling. The key to keeping a P in good balance is to eat on time and not get overheated. (It's that simple!)

P Digestion

The defining characteristic of the P Energy State is a very powerful digestive fire. The P Gut is programmed to naturally produce a strong appetite, which needs to be satisfied at particular times during the day. For instance, digestive power is strongest at noon, so it's very important for P Energy individuals to eat their largest meal at that time. When the P Gut is balanced, digestion is highly efficient; out of balance, the person may experience hyperacidity.

P Exercise

P Energy State individuals are extremely competitive and don't hold back. They have good stamina and strength, and are often drawn to organized sports. They are so goal-oriented that they naturally overdo exercise and pay the consequences later. P Energy State people need to avoid becoming overheated. Active water sports such as swimming, surfing, and parasailing are ideal.

P Sleep

A P person usually goes to sleep quickly and needs less sleep. When they are imbalanced, they may have difficulty sleeping.

K Energy State

K Energy State people tend to be steady and take some time to carefully consider any decision. They are not easily upset, and are often easygoing and agreeable. If they go out of balance, however, they can become stubborn and lack ambition. The key to keeping a K person in good balance is to keep them physically active and mentally stimulated.

K Digestion

Individuals with a K Energy State have a steady digestion and can miss a meal and be fine. Your K Energy State client usually loves food but needs to eat moderate amounts because they have a slower metabolism and gain weight easily. Of the three main types, Ks tend to drink the least amount of water.

<u>K Exercise</u>

K Energy State individuals tend to have good endurance and strength, but they need regular physical exercise to keep them from becoming lethargic and overweight. Running, jogging, and working out in the gym are all beneficial.

<u>K Sleep</u>

The K energy individuals have no trouble falling asleep but can have a hard time getting up in the morning, especially if they still need more rest.

VP (PV) Energy States

A VP Energy State person is similar to someone who has a PV Energy State, but it is important to note that whichever Energy State is listed first will tend to dominate. A VP person is quick, inspiring, and full of new ideas, but at the same time focused and ready to complete the project. VPs can be both energetic and sensitive. One side of them is in motion, while the other is goal-oriented.

When VPs are in good balance, they draw energy from their P qualities. When they are out of balance, their V qualities can cause them to become over-stimulated and quickly exhausted. This duality produces a reasonably strong but variable energy.

VP Digestion

The digestion of a VP is like their energy, strong but variable, and their appetite is good. Because their gut is partially V, they may be a picky or discriminating eater with strong preferences, and can be hungry one minute and not the next. Because their gut is also partially P, they need ample meals to sustain physical and mental activity. The presence of P indicates that it is especially important for VP individuals to eat on time. As a combination type, they have a more balanced appetite than people with a pure V or pure P Energy State.

When VPs are in good balance, they rarely have digestive problems. When out of balance, however, digestive issues can range from weak digestion to hyperactivity.

VP Exercise

VP Energy State people are agile and graceful and have good energy and strength.

VP Sleep

VP Energy individuals do not have a problem falling asleep unless they get over stimulated right before going to bed.

VK (KV) Energy State

This Energy State is an interesting combination of opposites. The V Energy State is light and airy, while the K Energy State is heavy and earthy. This combination of states indicates both steadiness and enthusiasm.

When VK is in good balance, the result is good health and physical stamina. When it is out of balance, VK people are prone to frequent colds and respiratory problems. With this particular energy state, it's important to remember that an imbalance of V will always push K out of balance, so V imbalances need to be addressed as soon as possible. VKs don't do well in cold or damp weather, and to avoid illness need to stay warm.

The VK combination gives rise to individuals who have a wide range of emotions. VKs are quick, inspiring, and full of new ideas, but at the same time they are stable, well liked, and methodical. VKs can be both grounded and sensitive. One part of them is in motion, while the other is steady and constant.

When out of balance, a VK person tends to be spacey, withdrawn, or even depressed. They may also obsess on issues, and become attached and/or anxious. It's especially good for VKs to have enjoyable social outings and stay rested, energized, and happy, in order to improve every aspect of their mind, body, and emotions.

VK Digestion

The digestion of a VK Energy State person (virtually the same as a KV Energy State person except that whichever energy state is listed first predominates), is generally strong and steady, and they enjoy an occasional snack. The V part of the VK combination makes the person a grazer with a constantly changing appetite, while the K part makes them love to eat. V and K complement each other when they are in balance. So, they enjoy food, but don't gain as much weight as pure K types.

When out of balance, their digestion slows down and they become more sensitive to what they eat.

VK Exercise

VK Energy State individuals have a mixture of opposite and can be both a sprinter and an endurance runner.

VK Sleep

The VK Energy individuals can fall asleep and stay asleep as long as their V Energy State is balanced.

PK (KP) Energy State

PK Energy State people have the hot, transformative qualities of a P Energy State plus the cool, stable qualities of a K Energy State. But if they don't stay in balance, they can boil over. PKs are generally large and strong. They might not be the star of the team, but they have the constitution to be a very good player.

A PK tends to be strong, sturdy, content, and easygoing. Their drive is steadied by their calm, easygoing nature. However, imbalances can cause impatience, anger, and lethargy. They can also become argumentative, stubborn, and withdrawn. It's very important for a PK, particularly, to maintain healthy family relationships and friendships in order to stay in good balance.

In the heat of the moment a PK might not think problems through completely. And if decisions backfire, they may be prone to useless regret. A PK individual will be happier and healthier if he or she spends more time listening and less time making assumptions and running scenarios in their head.

PK Digestion

The digestion and appetite of a PK Energy State person (which is virtually the same as KP, only P will predominate) are both strong. Anyone with a P gut has a good appetite. With a PK gut, they will have an even stronger appetite. PKs like to eat and can generally digest easily. However, because their gut is part K, their metabolism can slow down at times and they can have a hard time digesting greasy foods. Although it's easy for PKs to gain a few extra pounds, they can usually lose them without great effort.

When PKs are in good balance, they rarely have digestive problems. When out of balance, however, they must be aware of slower digestion and hyperacidity.

PK Exercise

PKs need to exercise daily. PKs have excellent stamina in activity, but have to be careful not to get overheated.

PK Sleep

The PK or KP individual generally falls asleep easily and gets a good sound sleep.

VPK Energy State or "Tri-Energy State"

This is a relatively rare mixture of the three types, and when in balance, it shows the best qualities of each. VPKs are often creative, motivated, steady, and good-natured. When they are in good balance, they tend to be in tune with their body and emotions, and can be intuitive. Physically strong with a moderate build, VPKs are usually in good health. They avoid most seasonal illnesses and experience only mild to moderate symptoms during each season (e.g. dry skin in the winter, some lethargy in the spring, and mild heat intolerance in the summer).

Life becomes complicated when one or more of their three Energy States goes out of balance. Often it is not clear which Energy State is first to go out of balance. Learn to "check in with yourself" and be alert to when something doesn't feel quite right. The best advice for VPKs is to treat imbalances in the following order: 1) Start with balancing V; 2) Go on to balance P; 3) Finally, address K. Keep in mind that it takes a VPK Energy State longer to come back into balance than other combinations of Energy States.

VPK Digestion

The digestion and appetite of a VPK Energy State person should be good. Since they have a stronger digestion than others, they can eat almost any kind of food and rarely experience excessive hunger or thirst. But because their symptoms are usually mild and somewhat veiled, it's hard to pinpoint how and when they go out of balance, so it's especially valuable for them to learn to listen to their body.

VPK Exercise

Since VPKs possess all three characteristics, any exercise is possible. The main thing is not to overdo it.

<u>VPK Sleep</u>

Because this is a part K Energy State, sleep is their friend. If they do go out of balance, it is usually the V Energy State, which might cause them sleep problems.

<u>Energy State Conclusion</u>

No single Energy State is better than another and each of us can rise to our full potential by staying in balance and achieving maximum levels of energy, performance, and success. For recommendations about specific Energy State diets, teas, spice mixes, and recipes, see *The Rest and Repair Diet: Heal Your Gut, Improve Your Physical and Mental Health, and Lose Weight,* and visit our website at docgut.com.

Quote from Basho

There are many different translations of this haiku. This one is by Makoto Ueda.

Energy State Quiz

This quiz is adapted from one which appears in *Dharma Parenting: Understand Your Child's Brilliant Brain for Greater Happiness, Health, Success, and Fulfillment* by Robert Keith Wallace, PhD and Fredrick Travis, PhD, Tarcher/Perigree, 2016

Chapter 4. TOTAL BRAIN COACHING

Musashi

There is more than one version of Musashi's famous sword battle on YouTube. The version we use is from the movie *The Samurai Trilogy.*

Total Brain Coaching

Total Brain Coaching is a system that effectively helps individuals, teams, and organizations change their habits. It starts with the understanding that each person, team, and organization, is different—with their own strengths and weakness, their own preferences and habits.

The book *Total Brain Coaching: A Holistic System of Effective Habit Change For the Individual, Team, and Organization* by Ted Wallace, MS, Robert Keith Wallace, Samantha Wallace, gives an in-depth description of the tools of Total Brain Coaching.

The Coherence Code

The 7 guiding principles of The Coherence Code that are the basis of Total Brain Coaching:

1. Discover Your Energy State : Once an individual, team, or organization decides to make a change, they need to deeply understand their own nature and habits, and how different external factors affect their inherent strengths and weaknesses.

2. Harness Your Neuroplasticity and Gut-Brain Axis: It is easier to create a new habit than to change an old one. Habits are like neural circuits, and establishing a new habit involves the creation of new wiring in the brain.

3. Use the Power of Attention: The easiest way to create a new habit is to use the power of attention to initiate small doable steps.

4. Finding Your Inner Rhythm: Each individual, team, or organization has its own inner rhythm. Being in tune with your rhythm makes it easier for you to incorporate a new habit into pre-existing routines.

5. Use the Feedback Matrix: For maximum coaching results, use reinforcement from four different coaching techniques.

6. Continuously Improve and Integrate: Each step of progress should be measured and evaluated. Quick feedback facilitates improvement and integration.

7. Celebrate Steps of Success

Recognize even small changes in habits and use positive reinforcement to celebrate every stage of achievement.

All of these principles are explained in detail in the book Total Brain Coaching and can be practically applied using specific tools such as delineating a personalized Habit Map and Plan according to their individual Energy State.

What you put your attention on grows stronger

We have taken this simple but profound quote from talks by Maharishi Mahesh Yogi. It is a concept which is expressed in many traditions. For example, there is a famous story is about two wolves who are in deadly conflict. One is cruel, negative, and destructive, while the other is kind, brave, and compassionate. The story ends with the question: which wolf wins? And the answer is, whichever wolf you feed or nourish! In other words, what you put your attention on grows stronger.

Mushin Quote

The quote on mushin is from an article by Aikido no Sekai, *Mushin: The Mind without Mind*, at https://aikidonosekai.wordpress.com/2014/03/23/aikido-mushin-no-mind/.

Kjell Enhager

Kjell Enhager is a coach in both business and sports. He has lectured to hundreds of thousands of people and has coached some of the biggest superstars and companies in his native Sweden and abroad. See *Quantum Golf: The Path to Golf Mastery* by Kjell Enhager and Samantha Wallace, Warner Books, New York, 1991

Triggers

Triggers: Creating Behavior That Lasts—Becoming the Person You Want to Be by Marshall Goldsmith and Mark Reiter, Crown Business, 2015

Quotes from Sun Tzu's *The Art of War*

This was taken from https://suntzusaid.com/ and is based on the english translation by Lionel Giles first published in 1910.

Chapter 5. THE ZEN GARDEN

Bushido

Bushido is a code of conduct and honor developed for the samurai way of life. It includes seven virtues: righteousness, courage, benevolence, respect, honesty, honor, duty, and self-control.

Way of the Warrior

This is Musashi's personal code explained in both his books, *The Book of Five Rings* and *The Way of Walking Alone*.

The Brush is the Sword of the Mind

This article by William Reed can be seen at the following site: https:// budojapan.com/feature-articles/the-brush-is-the-sword-of-the-mind%EF%BC%88miyamoto-musashi%EF%BC%89/.

Basho Quote

There are many different translations of this quote on the Internet.

Chapter 6. MORE COHERENT COMMUNICATION

Styles of communication

For details on how different Energy States communicate and interact, see the book *Total Brain Coaching: A Holistic System of Effective Habit Change For the Individual, Team, and Organization* by Ted Wallace, MS, Robert Keith Wallace, PhD, Samantha Wallace

Chapter 7. TOTAL BRAIN TEAM COACHING

Team coaching

For details on how to increase team coherence and performance, see the book *Total Brain Coaching: A Holistic System of Effective Habit Change For the Individual, Team, and Organization* by Ted Wallace, Robert Keith Wallace, PhD, Samantha Wallace

The Manifesto for Agile Software Development

The Manifesto for Agile Software Development includes the following 12 principles:

1. Our highest priority is to satisfy the customer
through early and continuous delivery
of valuable software.
2. Welcome changing requirements, even late in
development. Agile processes harness change for
the customer's competitive advantage.

3. Deliver working software frequently, from a couple of weeks to a couple of months, with a preference to the shorter timescale.

4. Business people and developers must work together daily throughout the project.

5. Build projects around motivated individuals. Give them the environment and support they need, and trust them to get the job done.

6. The most efficient and effective method of conveying information to and within a development team is face-to-face conversation.

7. Working software is the primary measure of progress.

8. Agile processes promote sustainable development. The sponsors, developers, and users should be able to maintain a constant pace indefinitely.

9. Continuous attention to technical excellence and good design enhances agility.

10. Simplicity—the art of maximizing the amount of work not done—is essential.

11. The best architectures, requirements, and designs emerge from self-organizing teams.

12. At regular intervals, the team reflects on how to become more effective, then tunes and adjusts its behavior accordingly.

Washington Crew 1936

The Boys in the Boat: Nine Americans and Their Epic Quest

for Gold at the 1936 Olympics by Daniel James Brown, Penguin Books, 2014

Chapter 8. TOTAL BRAIN DECISION MAKING

More on Ray Dalio's business practices

Please see the book *Principles* by Ray Dalio.

Mozart quote

There are different versions of this quote. See https://www.goodreads.com/author/quotes/22051.Wolfgang_Amadeus_Mozart

Einstein quote

This can be found at https://www.azquotes.com/quote/605671 and is attributed to Albert Einstein (2011). *Essays in Science*, p.11, Open Road Media

Recent brain research on intuition

A recent article on intuition is Zander T, Horr NK, Bolte A, Volz KG. Intuitive decision making as a gradual process: investigating semantic intuition-based and priming-based decisions with fMRI. *Brain Behav.* 2015;6(1):e00420. Published 2015 Dec 22. doi:10.1002/brb3.420

Chapter 9. IN THE ZONE

Agile and Fake Agile

There are a number of excellent articles written by Steve Denning in *Forbes* magazine, such as: *World Agility Forum Celebrates Excellence, Flays Fake Agile; Understanding Fake Agile;* and *How Amazon Became Agile.* He has also written the book *The Age of Agile: How Smart Companies Are Transforming the Way Work Gets Done* by Stephen Denning, Amacon, 2018.

Transcendental Meditation Program

The Transcendental Meditation technique is a unique, simple, and effective mental procedure. It takes about twenty minutes, twice each day, in which you sit comfortably with your eyes closed. It involves no belief or philosophy, no mood or lifestyle. Most people begin the technique for practical reasons, such as a desire for more energy or to decrease tension and anxiety. Over six million people of all ages, cultures, and religions have learned TM.

TM uses the natural tendency of the mind to spontaneously experience states of greater and greater happiness. The technique involves a real and measurable process of physiological refinement that utilizes the inherent capacity of the nervous system to refine its own functioning and unfold its full potential. During TM practice, your attention is very naturally and spontaneously drawn to quieter, more orderly states of mental activity until all mental activity is transcended, and you are left with no thoughts or sensations, only the experience of pure awareness itself. The result of the regular practice of TM is that your entire nervous system becomes rejuvenated and revitalized, and you become more successful and fulfilled in activity.

Extensive research documents the effectiveness of TM in improving both physical and mental health. TM produces a unique state of restful alertness (1-3, see references at end of section) with different brain wave patterns from other techniques of meditation (4). The practice of this technique helps every area of life by removing stress from the nervous system. Over 600 studies at more than 200 research institutes and universities have been conducted on the Transcendental Meditation program, and more than 380 of these studies have been published in peer-reviewed journals. [Note to Reader: "Peer-reviewed" means that scientists, whose qualifications and competencies are on similar level of accomplishment as those of the authors of the study, have evaluated the work. This method is the gold standard of science, employed to maintain the highest standard of quality and credibility.]

The US National Institutes of Health has awarded over $25 million to study the effects of TM on health, particularly on heart disease, the #1 killer in the US. One of the most significant studies found that African Americans with heart disease, who practiced the TM technique regularly, were 48% less likely to have a heart attack or stroke, or to die from other causes, compared with African Americans who simply attended a health education class. It is particularly interesting to note that researchers who conducted this study at the Medical College of Wisconsin in Milwaukee reported that the more regularly the patients meditated, the longer was their term of survival (5).

A number of important studies have shown that TM reduces high blood pressure (6). A statement from the American Heart Association concluded:

> The Transcendental Meditation technique is the only meditation practice that has been shown to lower blood pressure.
>
> Because of many negative studies or mixed results and a paucity of available trials, all other meditation techniques (including MBSR) received a 'Class III, no benefit, Level of Evidence C' recommendation. Thus, other meditation techniques are not recommended in clinical practice to lower BP at this time.
>
> "Transcendental Meditation practice is recommended for consideration in treatment plans for all individuals with blood pressure > 120/80 mm Hg.
>
> "Lower blood pressure through Transcendental Meditation practice is also associated with substantially reduced rates of death, heart attack, and stroke (7).

Research has shown that TM practice reduces cholesterol levels (8). Studies also show that meditators exhibit an improved ability to adapt to stressful situations (9,10) and a marked decrease in levels of plasma cortisol, commonly known as the "stress hormone" (11).

Research results in various areas of health document improvements in such conditions as asthma, diabetes, metabolic syndrome, pain, alcohol and drug abuse, and mental health (12-17).

In a five-year study on some 2000 individuals, researchers showed that TM meditators used medical and surgical health care services approximately one-half as often as did other insurance users. This study was conducted in cooperation with Blue Cross Blue Shield and controlled for other factors that might affect health care use, such as cost sharing, age, gender, geographic distribution, and profession. The TM subjects also showed a far lower rate of increase in health care utilization with increasing age (18).

In Québec, Canada, researchers compared the changes in physician costs for TM practitioners with those of non-practitioners over a five-year period. This study is particularly reliable because the Canadian government tracks health care costs closely for both meditators and the control group, due to Canada's national health care system. After the first year, the health care costs of the TM group decreased 11%, and after five years, their cumulative cost reduction was 28%. TM patients required fewer referrals, resulting in lower medical expenses for prescription drugs, tests, hospitalization, surgery, and other treatments (19).

Studies have documented how TM can slow and even reverse the aging process. One study showed that long-term TM meditators had a biological age roughly twelve years younger than their non-meditating counterparts (20). Researchers at Harvard University studied the effects of TM on mental health, behavioral flexibility, blood pressure, and longevity, in residents of homes for the elderly. The subjects were randomly assigned either to a no-treatment group or to one of three treatment programs: the TM program, mindfulness training, or a relaxation program.

Initially, all three groups were similar on pretest measures and expectancy of benefits, yet after only three months, the TM group showed significant improvements in cognitive functioning and blood pressure compared to the control groups. Reports from the TM subjects, compared to those of the mindfulness or the relaxation subjects, indicated that the TM practitioners felt more absorbed during their practice, and better and more relaxed immediately afterward. Overall, more TM subjects found their practice to be personally valuable than members of either of the control groups (21).

The most striking finding is that TM practice not only reverses age-related declines in overall health, but also directly enhances longevity. All the members of the TM group were still alive three years after the program began, in contrast to about only half of the members of the control groups. Research on the Transcendental Meditation program clearly shows that growing old no longer need signify a loss in the quality of life; rather, it can be an opportunity for further development (22-23). Scientists have suggested that one of the ways TM may improve health and increase longevity is by changing the expression of specific beneficial genes in our DNA (24-25).

Long-term changes in brain functioning have also been correlated with decreased stress-reactivity and neuroticism, and increased self-development, intelligence, learning ability, and self-actualization (26-30). One important psychological study on TM shows a significant decrease in levels of anxiety in TM practitioners as compared to subjects practicing other relaxation techniques (31). Studies in a variety of work and business settings show significantly increased productivity and efficiency (32-33).

TM is learned from a qualified TM teacher, and is taught in 7 steps, normally within a week's time according to your schedule. Most of the steps take 1-2 hours (though some are shorter). There is also a brief but important follow-up meeting 10 days after you learn the practice, and then once a month for the first three months after your TM course. All of these meetings are included in the course fee, along with lifelong support for your meditation program, including individual meditation checking, advanced meetings, and other special events.

Although there are a number of advanced TM programs, TM is always the core technique and will continue to benefit your life whether you choose to take an advanced program or not. (For more information on how to start TM, see TM.org.)

Selected References on Transcendental Meditation and Health

1. Wallace R.K. Physiological effects of Transcendental Meditation. *Science* 167:1751-1754, 1970

2. Wallace, R.K. et al. A wakeful hypometabolic physiologic state. *American Journal of Physiology* 221(3): 795-799, 1971

3. Wallace, R.K. Physiological effects of the Transcendental Meditation technique: A proposed fourth major state of consciousness. Ph.D. thesis. Physiology Department, University of California, Los Angeles, 1970

4. Travis, F.T. and Shear, J. Focused attention, open monitoring

and automatic self-transcending: Categories to organize meditations from Vedic, Buddhist and Chinese traditions. *Consciousness and Cognition* 19(4):1110-1118, 2010

5. Schneider R.H., et al. Stress Reduction in the Secondary Prevention of Cardiovascular Disease: Randomized, Controlled Trial of Transcendental Meditation and Health Education in Blacks. *Circ Cardiovasc Qual Outcomes* 5:750-758, 2012

6. Rainforth M.V., et al. Stress reduction programs in patients with elevated blood pressure: a systematic review and meta-analysis. *Current Hypertension Reports* 9:520–528, 2007

7. Brook R.D. et al., Beyond Medications and Diet: Alternative Approaches to Lowering Blood Pressure. A Scientific Statement from the American Heart Association. *Hypertension* 61(6):1360-83, 2013

8. Cooper M. J., et al. Transcendental Meditation in the management of hypercholesterolemia. *Journal of Human Stress* 5(4): 24–27, 1979

9. Orme-Johnson D.W. and Walton K. W. All approaches of preventing or reversing effects of stress are not the same. *American Journal of Health Promotion* 12:297-299, 1998

10. Barnes V. A., et al. Impact of Transcendental Meditation on cardiovascular function at rest and during acute stress in adolescents with high normal blood pressure. *Journal of Psychosomatic Research* 51: 597-605, 2001

11. Jevning R., et al. Adrenocortical activity during meditation.

Hormonal Behavior 10(1):54-60, 1978

12. Wilson A.F. et al. Transcendental Meditation and asthma. *Respiration* 32:74-80, 1975

13. Paul-Labrador M., et al. Effects of randomized controlled trial of Transcendental Meditation on components of the metabolic syndrome in subjects with coronary heart disease. *Archives of Internal Medicine* 166:1218-1224, 2006

14. Royer A. The role of the Transcendental Meditation technique in promoting smoking cessation: A longitudinal study. *Alcoholism Treatment Quarterly* 11: 219-236, 1994

15. Haratani T., et al. Effects of Transcendental Meditation (TM) on the mental health of industrial workers. *Japanese Journal of Industrial Health* 32: 656, 1990

16. Orme-Johnson D.W, et al. Neuroimaging of meditation's effect on brain reactivity to pain. *NeuroReport* 17(12):1359-63, 2006

17. Alexander C.N., et al. Treating and preventing alcohol, nicotine, and drug abuse through Transcendental Meditation: A review and statistical meta-analysis. *Alcoholism Treatment Quarterly* 11: 13-87, 1994.

18. Orme-Johnson D. W., Herron R. E. An Innovative Approach to Reducing Medical Care Utilization and Expenditures. *American Journal of Managed Care* 3: 135–144,1997

19. Herron R.E. Can the Transcendental Meditation Program

Reduce the Medical Expenditures of Older People? A Longitudinal Cost-Reduction Study in Canada. *Journal of Social Behavior and Personality* 17(1): 415–442, 2005

20. Wallace R.K., et al. The effects of the Transcendental Meditation and TM-Sidhi program on the aging process. *International Journal of Neuroscience* 16: 53-58, 1982

21. Alexander C.N., et al. Transcendental Meditation, mindfulness, and longevity. *Journal of Personality and Social Psychology* 57: 950-964, 1989

22. Alexander C.N., et al. The effects of Transcendental Meditation compared to other methods of relaxation in reducing risk factors, morbidity, and mortality. *Homeostasis* 35: 243-264, 1994

23. Schneider R.H., et al. Long-term effects of stress reduction on mortality in persons > 55 years of age with systemic hypertension. *American Journal of Cardiology* 95: 1060-1064, 2005

24. Duraimani S. et al. Effects of Lifestyle Modification on Telomerase Gene Expression in Hypertensive Patients: A Pilot Trial of Stress Reduction and Health Education Programs in African Americans. *PLOS ONE* 10(11): e0142689, 2015

25. Wenuganen, S. Anti-Aging Effects of the Transcendental Meditation Program: Analysis of Ojas Level and Global Gene Expression. Maharishi University of Management, ProQuest Dissertations Publishing, 3630467, 2014

26. Chandler H.M., et al. Transcendental Meditation and

postconventional self-development: A 10-year longitudinal study. *Journal of Social Behavior and Personality* 17(1): 93–121, 2005

27. Cranson R.W., et al. Transcendental Meditation and improved performance on intelligence-related measures: A longitudinal study. *Personality and Individual Differences* 12: 1105-1116, 1991

28. So K.T. and Orme-Johnson D.W. Three randomized experiments on the longitudinal effects of the Transcendental Meditation technique on cognition. *Intelligence* 29: 419-440, 2001

29. Tjoa A. Increased intelligence and reduced neuroticism through the Transcendental Meditation program. *Gedrag: Tijdschrift voor Psychologie* 3: 167-182, 1975

30. Alexander C.N., et al. Transcendental Meditation, self-actualization, and psychological health: A conceptual overview and statistical meta-analysis. *Journal of Social Behavior and Personality* 6: 189-247, 1991

31. Eppley K.R. et al. Differential effects of relaxation techniques on trait anxiety: A meta-analysis. *Journal of Clinical Psychology* 45: 957-974, 1989

32. Alexander C. N., et al. Effects of the Transcendental Meditation program on stress-reduction, health, and employee development: A prospective study in two occupational settings. *Stress, Anxiety and Coping* 6: 245–262, 1993

33. Harung H. S., et al. Peak performance and higher states of

consciousness: A study of world-class performers. *Journal of Managerial Psychology* 11(4): 3–23, 1996

Group Practice of TM and more Advanced Techniques

The collective consciousness of any company or any group of people is the sum of the consciousness of all of the individuals in that company or group. When the collective consciousness is incoherent, the company will almost certainly lack a clear mission and have many internal problems. When the collective consciousness is coherent, the company will have a unified mission—a clear intention of its purpose—and will demonstrate optimal teamwork and performance.

The concept of a collective consciousness which underlies and influences the structure of society has been expressed by many great thinkers. Some sophisticated sociological theories have vaguely described it as a social field or an interlocking network of social and behavioral interactions within specific economic and environmental conditions.

Maharishi Mahesh Yogi, founder of the Transcendental Meditation technique, was the first to encourage scientific research on the concept of collective consciousness. Many scientific papers, published in peer-reviewed journals, verify the practical application of Maharishi's concepts (see Chapter 11 notes). Many of the comments about the group dynamics of consciousness can be found in Maharishi's books.

In 1960, Maharishi predicted that one percent of a population practicing the Transcendental Meditation technique would produce measurable improvements in the quality of life for the whole population. This phenomenon was first studied in 1974 and was referred to as the "Maharishi Effect." In 1976, Maharishi brought out several advanced programs derived from the Vedic tradition, which greatly enhanced the Maharishi Effect. Scientists found that when even the square root of one percent of any population practices these programs in a group, there is a measurable marked reduction in violence and an improvement in the quality of life, a type of macroscopic field effect of coherence.

A large number of studies have documented the beneficial effects of the practice of TM and its advanced programs on reducing crime and violence and improving the quality of life in different areas of the world. One demonstration project was conducted in 1993 in Washington, DC, by Dr. John Hagelin and colleagues. An independent panel of more than twenty sociologists, criminologists, and members of the Washington, DC government and police department advised on the study design and reviewed the analysis of the findings. The study included over 4000 people gathered in Washington to participate in a "peace assembly," practicing TM and specific related advanced programs for extended periods. Results showed that as the group size increased, there was a highly significant decrease in violent crime.

A remarkable aspect of this study was that it took place in August, when the weather is especially hot in Washington, DC. In fact, the police chief of Washington, who sat on the independent board of researchers monitoring the project, said in an interview, "The only way this group can lower crime by 20 percent in

Washington in August is if we have two feet of snow!" In fact, the meditating group lowered crime by 23.6 percent.

How could such a thing happen? The individuals in the group didn't go out on the streets and physically stop people from committing crimes. They simply meditated quietly together in various locations around the city. The coherence effect which they created in the collective consciousness of the city was similar to the result of throwing a pebble in a pond: Ripples of higher, more coherent waves of consciousness went out in all directions, creating sufficient coherence in the collective consciousness of the city so that crime was spontaneously reduced.

Research demonstrates that it is possible to influence the collective consciousness of society through the group practice of the TM technique and its advanced programs.

Selected References on Group Dynamics of Consciousness

1. Hagelin, J.S., et al. Effects of group practice of the Transcendental Meditation program on preventing violent crime in Washington, DC: results of the National Demonstration Project, June-July 1993. *Social Indicators Research* 47: 153-201, 1999

2. Orme-Johnson, D.W., et al. International peace project in the Middle East: The effect of the Maharishi Technology of the Unified Field. *Journal of Conflict Resolution* 32: 776–812, 1988

3. Orme-Johnson, D.W., et al. The long-term effects of the

Maharishi Technology of the Unified Field on the quality of life in the United States (1960 to 1983). *Social Science Perspectives Journal* 2:127-146, 1988

4. Orme-Johnson, D.W., et al. Preventing terrorism and international conflict: Effects of large assemblies of participants in the Transcendental Meditation and TM-Sidhi programs. *Journal of Offender Rehabilitation* 36: 283–302, 2003

5. Brown, C.L. Overcoming barriers to use of promising research among elite Middle East policy groups. *Journal of Social Behavior and Personality* 17:489-546, 2005

6. Cavanaugh, K.L. Time series analysis of U.S. and Canadian inflation and unemployment: A test of a field-theoretic hypothesis. *Proceedings of the American Statistical Association, Business and Economics Statistics Section* (Alexandria, VA: American Statistical Association): 799–804, 1987

7. Cavanaugh, K.L. and King, K.D. Simultaneous transfer function analysis of Okun's misery index: Improvements in the economic quality of life through Maharishi's Vedic Science and technology of consciousness. *Proceedings of the American Statistical Association, Business and Economics Statistics Section* (Alexandria, VA: American Statistical Association): 491–496, 1988

8. Davies, J.L. Alleviating political violence through enhancing coherence in collective consciousness. Dissertation Abstracts International 49(8): 2381A, 1989

9. Gelderloos, P. et al. The dynamics of US–Soviet relations, 1979–1986: Effects of reducing social stress through the Transcendental Meditation and TM-Sidhi program. *Proceedings of the Social Statistics Section of the American Statistical Association* (Alexandria, VA: American Statistical Association): 297–302, 1990

10. Dillbeck, M.C. Test of a field theory of consciousness and social change: Time series analysis of participation in the TM-Sidhi program and reduction of violent death in the U.S. *Social Indicators Research* 22: 399–418, 1990

11. Assimakis, P.D. and Dillbeck, M.C. Time series analysis of improved quality of life in Canada: Social change, collective consciousness, and the TM-Sidhi program. *Psychological Reports* 76: 1171–1193, 1995

12. Hatchard, G.D. et al. A model for social improvement. Time series analysis of a phase transition to reduced crime in Merseyside metropolitan area. *Psychology, Crime, and Law* 2: 165–174, 1996

13. Dillbeck, M.C. et al. The Transcendental Meditation program and crime rate change in a sample of forty-eight cities. *Journal of Crime and Justice* 4: 25–45, 1981

14. Dillbeck, M.C. et al. Test of a field model of consciousness and social change: The Transcendental Meditation and TM-Sidhi program and decreased urban crime. *The Journal of Mind and Behavior* 9: 457–486, 1988

15. Dillbeck, M.C. et al. Consciousness as a field: The Transcendental Meditation and TM-Sidhi program and changes in social indicators. *The Journal of Mind and Behavior* 8: 67–104, 1987.

David Lynch Foundation

The David Lynch Foundation for Consciousness-Based Education and World Peace is a global charitable foundation founded by film director David Lynch to prevent and eradicate trauma and stress among at-risk populations through promoting widespread implementation of the evidence-based Transcendental Meditation program in order to improve their health, cognitive capabilities and performance in life.

At-risk populations suffer from epidemic levels of chronic stress and stress-related disorders—fueling violence, crime, and soaring health costs, and compromising the effectiveness of education, health, rehabilitation and vocational programs now in place. Since its founding in 2005, the David Lynch Foundation, a 501(c)(3) organization, has helped to bring the stress-reducing Transcendental Meditation technique to more than 500,000 children and adults around the world. The Foundation focuses on underserved inner-city students; veterans with PTSD and their families; and women and children who are survivors of violence and abuse.

The David Lynch Foundation has organized and hosted scientific and professional conferences on business, education, veterans, corrections, and rehabilitation as well as town hall meetings to educate leaders and the general public in the benefits of Transcendental Meditation. In addition, the Foundation funds university and medical school research to assess the effects of the program on academic performance, ADHD and other learning disorders, anxiety, depression, substance abuse, cardiovascular disease, post-traumatic stress disorder, and diabetes.

The Foundation has worked with other private foundations and government agencies, including the National Institutes of Health, General Motors Foundation, the Chrysler Foundation, the Kellogg Foundation, the American Indian Education Association, and Indian Health Services, along with numerous school districts and state departments of corrections.

[Note to Reader: The TM program has been endorsed and supported by a number of well-known individuals including Tom Hanks, Martin Scorsese, Ellen DeGeneres, Jerry Seinfeld, Paul McCartney, George Stephanopoulos, Katy Perry, and Hugh Jackman, among others.]

Chapter 10. SAMURAI NEGOTIATION

The material covered in the Total Brain Coaching Workshops is described in the book *Total Brain Coaching: A Holistic System of Effective Habit Change For the Individual, Team, and Organization* by Ted Wallace, MS, Robert Keith Wallace, PhD, Samantha Wallace.

Chapter 11. THE COHERENCE EFFECT

In Tune with Nature

Support of nature is expressed by Maharishi as an innocent spontaneous alignment with the infinite power of nature. There are various tools which can create support of nature for an individual, company, or team. These include: the TM technique, the group practice of TM and its more advanced techniques, and the application of specific Vedic technologies.

RECOMMENDATIONS

Meditation

Everybody knows that meditation helps people deal with stress, but which kind of meditation is best for you? Recent research clearly shows that different types of meditation are not the same. There are three main categories of meditation procedure, each with different effects on the brain:

- Focused Attention (including Zen, compassion, qigong, and vipassana): gamma (fast) EEG indicates that the brain is concentrated and focused.

- Open Monitoring (including mindfulness and Kriya yoga): theta (slow) EEG indicates that the mind is in a more contemplative state, following its own internal mental processes.

- Automatic self-transcending (including Transcendental Meditation): coherent alpha1 (foundational) EEG indicates that the mind is in a unique state of restful alertness.

The first two types of meditation construct mental tools to help us cope with life. Generally speaking, Focused Attention meditations train the mind to concentrate more closely and for longer periods. Open Monitoring meditations, which include many techniques of mindfulness, help us develop greater awareness of our body (such as our breathing patterns), and cultivate insight into what we are thinking and doing.

Automatic Self-Transcending meditations are fundamentally different because they do not involve thinking about something—rather, they allow the mind to settle down to a very quiet state while becoming more alert. The goal of Transcendental Meditation is not to develop a specific mental ability, such as improved concentration, but rather to improve the mind's basic functioning by making it more settled and alert. The word "transcend" means to go beyond, and when we transcend during TM we go beyond thoughts and categories—we are, in effect, stepping outside the boundaries of our problems. After our TM practice, we come back to our situation better able to see the big picture and find creative solutions.

Because we have experienced—personally, and, in the case of Dr. R.K. Wallace, as a researcher—how effective Transcendental Meditation is, Total Brain Coaching focuses on the Transcendental Meditation technique. (See Notes in Chapter 9, and TM.org for more details on TM.)

Yoga

Yoga has long been recognized as a method to improve and maintain your body while you are on the path to health, happiness, success, fulfillment, and, ultimately, enlightenment. Research shows that yoga postures or asanas improve certain psychological conditions, including anxiety and depression, and provide health benefits for those with high blood pressure, various pain syndromes, and immune disorders.

Choose whichever form of yoga best suits your individual Energy State, age, and needs. We recommend the Maharishi Yoga Asana program because it is especially respectful of your body and your consciousness, and supports the experience of transcendence.

Beauty

Former model Samantha Wallace, Robert Keith Wallace, PhD, and Veronica Butler, MD have written *Beauty And Being Yourself: A User-Friendly Introduction to Ayurveda and Essential Oil Skincare*. *Beauty And Being Yourself* includes a quiz to determine your True Skin Type and explains how understanding your True Skin Type gives you an extraordinary guide to caring for your skin, your health, and your inner and outer beauty at any age.

After reading this book, you can look at the label of any skin product and be able to answer the following:

- Does it contain oils that are good for my particular skin?
- Are the Essential Oils listed worth the price?
- Are there any chemicals I should check for toxicity?

Parenting

Dharma Parenting: Understand Your Child's Brilliant Brain

for Greater Happiness, Health, Success, and Fulfillment by Robert Keith Wallace, PhD, and Fredrick Travis, PhD helps you understand how to simply and effectively make use of both contemporary science and ancient Ayurvedic knowledge to raise a happy and successful child.

The first tool of Dharma Parenting is to determine your child's, and your own, Brain/Body type (what we call Energy State in this book) through a simple quiz. The Brain/Body type or Energy State helps you understand why one child learns quickly and forgets quickly, while another learns slowly and forgets slowly; why one child is hyperactive and another is calm and steady; or why one falls asleep quickly while another takes hours to fall asleep. Dharma Parenting offers unique insight into such areas of universal parental concern as: emotions, behavior, language, learning styles, diet, health, and the important parent-child relationship.

The Gut-Brain Connection

One of the most important achievements of modern science is the discovery of the gut-brain connection. This complex network called the gut-brain axis has an enormous impact on the health of your body and mind. The gut-brain axis consists of a number of major physiological systems: the nervous system, enteric nervous system or ENS, endocrine system, immune system, and the gut bacteria or microbiome.

The microbiome is technically defined as all of the microorganisms that live in you or on you—including their genetic material.

The vast majority of these microorganisms, however, are the 30 trillion friendly bacteria that live in your lower gut.

We used to believe that all bacteria were harmful. And while it's true that certain virulent bacteria and viruses are capable of killing millions of people, it turns out that most of the bacteria living in your gut are wonderfully beneficial. There is a two-way communication between the gut and the brain. Stress in your brain can disrupt your digestive process, while stress in your gut can disrupt your mind and emotions.

Gut bacteria use the vagus nerve to communicate with your brain, and also produce a wide variety of chemical messengers, including neurotransmitters and hormones that can enter the bloodstream and affect parts of your brain. Brain imaging has shown that people react differently to stress, depending on the type of bacteria in their gut. Subjects receiving a probiotic showed a reduced stress response, with less activity in the emotional areas of the brain.

By understanding the connection between the brain and the gut, we can better understand the basic principles of ancient systems of health such as Ayurveda. These natural systems of health place a great emphasis on improving digestion and removing toxins from the body.

Hippocrates, considered to be the father of Western medicine, said, "All disease begins in the gut." In the past, doctors used to consider this a strange concept, but now most doctors and scientists understand that your gut bacteria have an enormous impact on both your mind and body, and that they may be key to the treatment of many disorders and diseases—from diabetes to Alzheimer's, even obesity. The state of your health depends upon the state of your digestion and gut bacteria.

The problem is that many people have adopted bad habits, which disrupt the gut and can eventually lead to chronic disease. Your gut needs a chance to rest and repair itself and to re-enliven your own inner intelligence. This may sound simplistic, but it works. Rest enables your body's repair systems to kick in and begin to heal and re-establish balance in your gut. Fatigue is the enemy.

To improve the health of the gut we have developed a specific diet, which combines the ancient knowledge of Ayurveda with the latest findings of modern medicine. This diet is called The Rest and Repair Diet and in addition to improving digestion and gut bacteria it also helps to promote clearer awareness so that you can make other positive changes in your lifestyle and activities.

For more details on this program see *The Rest And Repair Diet: Heal Your Gut, Improve Your Physical and Mental Health, and Lose Weight* by Robert Keith Wallace, PhD, Samantha Wallace, Andrew Stenberg, MA, Jim Davis, DO, and Alexis Farley, Dharma Publications, 2019.

For more information on the microbiome and gut bacteria see *Gut Crisis: How Diet, Probiotics, and Friendly Bacteria Help You Lose Weight and Heal Your Body and Mind* by Robert Keith Wallace, PhD, and Samantha Wallace, Dharma Publications, 2017.

Training in Maharishi AyurVeda

Maharishi AyurVeda is a revival of Ayurveda, which includes consciousness-based approaches to health as well as an advanced methodology of pulse diagnosis. Maharishi University of Management (MUM) was founded by Maharishi Mahesh Yogi, who is also the founder of the Transcendental Meditation technique, and Maharishi AyurVeda. MUM offers an online Master of Science degree in Maharishi AyurVeda and Integrative Medicine. The program is a 3-year part-time online program, which integrates the ancient knowledge of Ayurveda with what has been discovered by modern medicine. It is taught by qualified doctors, and students are given in-residence clinical training by Maharishi AyurVeda experts for two weeks each year. MUM is a member of the National Ayurvedic Medical Association and is accredited by the Higher Learning Commission. MUM also offers an online and in-residence BA in Ayurveda Wellness and Integrative Health. See mum.edu for more details.

REFERENCES

Useful Websites

Totalbraincoaching.com

TM.org

MUM.edu

Useful Books

Total Brain Coaching: A Holistic System of Effective Habit Change For the Individual, Team, and Organization by Ted Wallace, MS, Robert Keith Wallace, PhD, and Samantha Wallace, Dharma Publications, 2020

The Book of Five Rings by Miyamoto Musashi, Bottom of the Hill Publishing, 2010

Musashi's Dokkodo (The Way of Walking Alone): Half Crazy, Half Genius—Finding Modern Meaning in the Sword Saint's Last Words. Kindle Edition by Miyamoto Musashi, Lawrence Kane (Editor), Kris Wilder (Editor), Alain Burrese (Editor), Lisa Christensen (Editor), Wallace Smedley (Editor), Dan Anderson (Foreword), Stickman Publications, Inc., 2015

Hit Refresh: The Quest to Rediscover Microsoft's Soul and Imagine a Better Future for Everyone by Satya Nadella, Greg Shaw, Jill Tracie Nichols, HarperBusiness, 2017

Principles by Ray Dalio, Simon & Schuster, 2017

Evolvagility: Growing an Agile Leadership Culture from the Inside by Michael Hamman, Agile Leadership Institute, 2019

Coaching Agile Teams: A Companion for Scrum Masters, Agile Coaches, and Project Managers in Transition by Lyssa Adkins, Addison-Wesley, 2010

The Age of Agile: How Smart Companies Are Transforming the Way Work Gets Done by Stephen Denning, Amacon, 2018

Mindset: The New Psychology of Success by Carol S. Dweck, Ballantine Books, 2007

Triggers: Creating Behavior That Lasts—Becoming the Person You Want to Be by Marshall Goldsmith and Mark Reiter, Crown Business, 2015

The Boys in the Boat: Nine Americans and Their Epic Quest for Gold at the 1936 Olympics by Daniel James Brown, Penguin Books, 2014

Success from Within: Discovering the Inner State that Creates Personal Fulfillment and Business Success by Jay B. Marcus, MUM Press, 1990

Enlightened Management: Building High-Performance People by Gerald Swanson and Bob Oates, MUM Press, 1987

Quantum Golf: The Path to Golf Mastery by Kjell Enhager and Samantha Wallace, Warner Books, New York, 1991

Gut Crisis: How Diet, Probiotics, and Friendly Bacteria Help You Lose Weight and Heal Your Body and Mind by Robert Keith Wallace, PhD, and Samantha Wallace, Dharma Publications, 2017

The Rest And Repair Diet: Heal Your Gut, Improve Your Physical and Mental Health, and Lose Weight by Robert Keith Wallace, PhD, Samantha Wallace, Andrew Stenberg, MA, Jim Davis, DO, and Alexis Farley, Dharma Publications, 2019

Dharma Parenting: Understand Your Child's Brilliant Brain for Greater Happiness, Health, Success, and Fulfillment by Robert Keith Wallace, PhD, and Fredrick Travis, PhD, Tarcher/Perigree, 2016

Beauty And Being Yourself: A User-Friendly Introduction to Ayurveda And Essential Oil Skincare by Samantha Wallace, Robert Keith Wallace, PhD, Veronica Butler, MD, Dharma Publications, 2020

Science of Being and Art of Living: Transcendental Meditation by Maharishi Mahesh Yogi, MUM Press, Kindle edition, 2011

Maharishi's Absolute Theory of Government by Maharishi Mahesh Yogi, MUM Press, 1995

Maharishi Mahesh Yogi on the Bhagavad-Gita, A New Translation and Commentary, Chapters 1-6, MUM Press, 2016

Strength in Stillness: The Power of Transcendental Meditation by Bob Roth, Simon & Schuster, 2018

Catching the Big Fish: Meditation, Consciousness, and Creativity by David Lynch, Tarcher/Penguin 2007

An Introduction to Transcendental Meditation: Improve Your Brain Functioning, Create Ideal Health, and Gain Enlightenment Naturally, Easily, Effortlessly by Robert Keith Wallace, PhD, and Lincoln Akin Norton, Dharma Publications, 2016

Transcendental Meditation: A Scientist's Journey to Happiness, Health, and Peace, Adapted and Updated from The Physiology of Conscious-ness: Part 1 by Robert Keith Wallace, PhD, Dharma Publications, 2016

The Neurophysiology of Enlightenment: How the Transcendental Med-itation and TM-Sidhi Program Transform the Functioning of the Hu-man Body, by Robert Keith Wallace, PhD, Dharma Publications, 2016

Maharishi Ayurveda and Vedic Technology: Creating Ideal Health for the Individual and World, Adapted and Updated from The Physiology of Consciousness: Part 2 by Robert Keith Wallace, PhD, Dharma Pub-lications, 2016

In Balance leben: Wie wir trotz Stress mit unserer Energie richtig umge-hen Broschiert (Translation: *Living in Balance: How to deal with our energy properly despite stress.*) by Dr. med. Ulrich Bauhofer, Südwest Verlag, 2013

Index